Sri Guru

English in Business Field and IT Sector

YouTube Channel: **Sri Guru Academy**

TITLE OF THE BOOK	:	**English in Business Field and IT Sector**
AUTHOR	:	**Thanga Durai** M.A., M.Phil.,
FIRST EDITION	:	2026
PAGES	:	168
PRICE	:	250
ISBN NUMBER	:	978-81-998152-4-7
PUBLISHER	:	**Sri Guru Publication**
(Imprint)		Madurai
Cell & WhatsApp	:	75300 08201
EMAIL ID	:	srigurupub@gmail.com
PRINTER	:	**Sree Meenakshi Printers** Madurai

Importance of English in Business

International Communication
Most global companies use English to communicate with clients, partners, and employees.

Business Meetings & Presentations
English helps professionals express ideas, strategies, and reports clearly.

Email & Report Writing
Business emails, proposals, and reports are usually written in English.

Negotiation & Deals
Strong English skills help in convincing clients and finalizing contracts.

Career Growth
Good English increases chances of promotions, overseas opportunities, and better salaries.

Networking
Conferences, seminars, and professional platforms (like LinkedIn) mainly use English.

Learning & Research
Most business books, journals, and case studies are in English.

1. SELF INTRODUCTION

Name

- My name is John.
- I am Kevin.
- Everyone calls me Rohan.
- Please call me Anand.
- You can call me Akshaya.

Place

- I am from Delhi.
- I hail from….
- I come from Mumbai.
- I was born in London.
- I live in Manchester.
- I reside in Delhi.
- I grew up in Chennai.
- I live in Portland Street.
- I spent most of my life in Bristol.

Age

- I am 22 years old.
- I am 24.
- I am over/almost/nearly 30.

Marital status

- I am married.
- I am single.
- I am divorced.

- I am engaged.
- I have a wife.
- I am a widow.
- I am a widower.
- I am still looking for one.
- I have two children.
- I don't have children.

Family

- There are five people in my family.
- My family has four people.
- I live with my parents.
- I am the only child
- I have a brother and a sister.
- I have two brothers and both of them work in different MNCs.
- My father is a Businessman.
- My father is working in a Private Company.
- My father is retired Government Employee.
- My mother is a Homemaker.

Job / Qualification

- I am a Teacher.
- I am unemployed.
- I am looking for a job.
- I have three years experience in Private Company.
- I have been working in Bangalore for 6 years.
- I am a fresher so I have no work experience.
- I am a student of Oxford University.
- I have done my schooling in St. John High School.

- I have completed my MCA in Wales University.
- I am pursuing Bachelor of Business in Marketing.
- I have completed my Master of Business in Marketing.
- I did my MBA in Cambridge University.
- I have secured 75% of mark in BBA.

Hobby

- I like action movies.
- My hobbies are painting and surfing net.
- I love watching football.
- My hobby is reading.
- My hobbies are playing with friends, listening to music and shopping.
- In my free time, I like painting.

Strength / Weakness

- My strength is I can adopt any type of environment.
- My strength is I am a fast learner.
- I have good leadership skill.
- I am friendly in nature.
- I am adaptable to any kind of situation.
- I am a kind of helping tendency.
- I can work hard and achieve my targets in time.
- My weakness is I am not comfortable, until I finish my work in time.
- My short-term goal is to get the job in reputed company.
- My long-term goal is to become a Business magnet.

2. GREETINGS

- How are you?
- How do you do?
- How is everything?
- How is it going?
- How is your business?
- How about you?
- How are the things going?
- I am happy to see you again. How are you?

*RESPONSE TO **HOW ARE YOU***

- Fine.
- I am fine. Thanks.
- Pretty good.
- It's going well.
- Not bad.
- I am good.
- It's the same as always.

WELCOME

- You are welcome.
- Whoever wants to join our club will be welcome.
- Welcome to the club.
- I am so happy you could visit.
- You are welcome to join us.
- I am delighted to have you here.
- I am so glad you could come.
- Welcome back.

THANK YOU

- Thanks for waiting.
- Thank you for understanding me.
- Thank you for your attention.
- Thank you for your patience.
- Thank you for helping me.
- Thank you for your time.
- Thanks for your help.
- Thank you for reminding me.
- Thanks for your effort.
- Thanks for your advice.
- Thank you for replying to my email.
- Thank you for the lift.
- Thank you for invitation me to the dinner.
- Thanks for the gift.
- Thank you for inviting me.
- Thank you for coming.
- I am so grateful for your support.
- Thank you, I will try that.

*RESPONSE TO **THANK YOU***

- My pleasure.
- You are welcome.
- It is my pleasure.
- No problem.
- I am glad to help you.
- I am happy to help.
- I am here to help.
- Don't worry about it.

CONGRATULATION

- Congratulation!
- That's incredible.
- Happy journey.
- You are doing a great job.
- That was first class work.
- You are doing well.
- I wish you luck.
- Best of luck.
- Hope all goes well.
- Best wishes for you.

GOODBYE

- Goodbye!
- Take care.
- Keep in touch.
- Bye Bye! See you.
- See you on Sunday.
- See you again.
- Please convey my regards to your parents.

3. GLAD TO MEET YOU

- Nice to see you again.
- How wonderful to meet you!
- It is a pleasure to meet you.
- It was nice talking to you.
- Great interacting with you.
- It is good to see you again.

4. INTRODUCTION

- John, this is Michael.
- Adam, have you met Sophia.
- This is Albert. He works with me.
- This is my friend John.
- I just wanted to introduce myself. I am Sam.
- Tom, I would like you to meet Lucy.
- This is Daisy.
- Let me introduce myself. My name is Smith.
- Tom, let me introduce you to Maria.
- David, I would like to introduce you to Henry.
- Please go around and introduce yourself to anyone.
- Jack, allow me to introduce you to Michael.

5. YOU SEEM FAMILIAR

- I know you from somewhere.
- Have we met before?
- You seem familiar.
- I am sure I have seen you before.
- I don't think we have met before.
- I think we have met before.
- You look like someone I know.

6. PLACE

- Where do you live?
- Where are you staying?
- Where is your home?
- Where are you from?

- Where do you stay?
- Which is your native place?
- Where is your office?
- I live in Bangalore.
- I am from Delhi.
- My native place is Chennai.
- I come from Mumbai.

7. BASIC INTERVIEW QUESTIONS

- What is your qualification?
- What is your educational qualification?
- Tell me about yourself.
- Please introduce yourself.
- What are your strengths?
- What are your weaknesses?
- What are your short term goals?
- What are your long-term goals?
- What are your Career Goals?
- What do you want to become?
- Why do you want to join this company?
- Why do you want to leave your current job?
- What are you currently doing?
- Why did you leave your previous job?
- Why do you want to work in this company?
- Where do you see yourself four or five years?
- How much salary do you expect?
- How do you feel about working nights/weekends?
- Are you comfortable with rotational shifts?
- Tell me your positive and negative points.

- Can you work under pressure?
- Tell me about a difficult situation you have faced.
- Why should we hire you?
- Why should I hire you?
- What does success mean to you?
- What type of person are you?
- What are your Salary Requirements?
- Is your wife employed?
- Are you married?
- Where do you come from?
- What is your aim in life?
- What is your hobby?
- Have you any previous experience?
- What is the difference between hard work and smart work?
- Could you tell us something about yourself?
- If you could change one thing about your personality, what would it be…
- Do you work on Sundays?
- Are you working anywhere at present?
- Reason behind leaving your last job?
- Why are you looking for a job change?
- Why have you been unemployed for such as long time?
- Why do you want to do work with our company?
- How do you think you are fit for the job?
- Do you have any question for me?
- Do you have any question to ask me?

8. BUSINESS LANGUAGE

Business Communication

- I have a business idea.
- I want to start a company.
- I sell products online.
- I provide services.
- My business is small.
- I work every day.
- I need more customers.
- I make a plan.
- I set a goal.
- I work hard.
- I earn money.
- I save money.
- I invest money.
- I learn new skills.
- I solve problems.
- I talk to customers.
- I answer emails.
- I promote my business.
- I use social media.
- I build my brand.
- I sell good products.
- I offer quality service.
- Customers trust me.
- I keep improving.
- I manage my time.
- I work with a team.

- I lead my team.
- I hire people.
- I train employees.
- I pay salaries.
- I create value.
- I help people.
- I take risks.
- I face challenges.
- I stay motivated.
- I stay focused.
- I follow my dreams.
- I never give up.
- I learn from mistakes.
- I grow every day.
- I check my sales.
- I track my expenses.
- I manage my budget.
- I reduce costs.
- I increase profits.
- I find new ideas.
- I test my ideas.
- I launch products.
- I listen to feedback.
- I improve my service.
- I talk to investors.
- I explain my idea.
- I build a website.
- I design a logo.
- I choose a name.

- I register my business.
- I follow rules.
- I pay taxes.
- I manage accounts.
- I check reports.
- I meet clients.
- I close deals.
- I sign contracts.
- I grow slowly.
- I stay patient.
- I stay positive.
- I think big.
- I act fast.
- I plan ahead.
- I stay organized.
- I learn marketing.
- I learn sales.
- I learn finance.
- I learn leadership.
- I improve daily.
- I work smart.
- I stay strong.
- I take action.
- I stay confident.
- I build connections.
- I meet new people.
- I share ideas.
- I ask questions.
- I give solutions.

- I solve customer problems.
- I build trust.
- I grow my network.
- I stay creative.
- I try new things.
- I adapt quickly.
- I learn from others.
- I read books.
- I watch videos.
- I attend meetings.
- I join events.
- I seek advice.
- I accept feedback.
- I improve my product.
- I stay disciplined.
- I stay committed.
- I focus on growth.
- I improve quality.
- I help my team.
- I guide my team.
- I respect customers.
- I value time.
- I plan my day.
- I set priorities.
- I finish tasks.
- I track progress.
- I avoid waste.
- I improve systems.
- I create systems.

- I stay efficient.
- I manage stress.
- I stay calm.
- I stay productive.
- I build habits.
- I stay consistent.
- I focus on results.
- I measure success.
- I fix problems.
- I take responsibility.
- I lead by example.
- I support my team.
- I celebrate wins.
- I stay humble.
- I keep learning.
- I stay curious.
- I grow my business.
- I improve every day.
- I believe in myself.
- I trust my vision.
- I stay dedicated.
- I build something great.
- I create opportunities.
- I help others succeed.
- I stay inspired.
- I take initiative.
- I work with passion.
- I stay flexible.
- I manage risks.

- I find solutions.
- I act quickly.
- I think clearly.
- I stay focused.
- I stay driven.
- I move forward.
- I build success.
- I never stop learning.
- I am working on a new business idea.
- I want to expand my company.
- I am improving my product quality.
- I am building a strong team.
- I am learning new business strategies.
- My goal is to grow my business globally.
- I am focusing on customer satisfaction.
- I am developing a marketing plan.
- I am testing new business ideas.
- I am analyzing market trends.
- I am trying to understand customer needs.
- I am creating value for my customers.
- I am building long-term relationships.
- I am improving my communication skills.
- I am managing my finances carefully.
- I am working on increasing my profits.
- I am reducing unnecessary expenses.
- I am exploring new opportunities.
- I am planning to launch a new product.
- I am building a personal brand.
- I am learning from successful entrepreneurs.

- I am reading business books regularly.
- I am attending business seminars.
- I am improving my leadership skills.
- I am working on time management.
- I believe consistency is the key to success.
- I always try to learn from my failures.
- I focus on solving real-world problems.
- I believe in continuous improvement.
- I always look for new business opportunities.
- I am developing a strong work ethic.
- I try to stay productive throughout the day.
- I focus on building a sustainable business.
- I try to deliver the best value to customers.
- I believe customer feedback is very important.
- I regularly review my business performance.
- I try to improve my decision-making skills.
- I focus on long-term growth.
- I avoid short-term thinking.
- I believe in smart investments.
- I am building systems to improve efficiency.
- I am automating repetitive tasks.
- I am improving my negotiation skills.
- I am focusing on business scalability.
- I am learning how to manage risks effectively.
- I believe teamwork is essential for success.
- I always try to motivate my team.
- I focus on building a positive work culture.
- I believe leadership requires responsibility.
- I am working on becoming a better leader.

- I strive to build a scalable and sustainable business model.
- I continuously analyze market trends to stay ahead of competitors.
- I believe innovation is the key driver of long-term success.
- I focus on creating solutions that address real customer pain points.
- I aim to deliver exceptional value through my products and services.
- I am constantly refining my strategies based on data and feedback.
- I believe calculated risks are necessary for business growth.
- I prioritize long-term vision over short-term profits.
- I focus on building a strong and recognizable brand identity.
- I invest in continuous learning and skill development.
- I believe adaptability is crucial in a rapidly changing market.
- I leverage technology to improve business efficiency.
- I focus on building strong professional networks.
- I believe leadership is about inspiring others.
- I emphasize the importance of accountability in my team.
- I aim to create a positive impact through my business.
- I believe customer satisfaction drives business success.
- I use data-driven decisions to guide my strategy.
- I constantly seek ways to optimize my operations.
- I focus on delivering consistent quality.
- I believe resilience is essential for overcoming business challenges.
- I focus on building long-term customer loyalty.
- I invest in innovation to stay competitive.
- I encourage creativity within my team.
- I prioritize transparency in my business practices.

- I aim to create a culture of continuous improvement.
- I believe strong leadership builds strong organizations.
- I focus on aligning my team with my vision.
- I measure success through impact and growth.
- I continuously refine my business processes.
- I strive to balance profitability with sustainability.
- I believe ethical business practices lead to long-term success.
- I aim to create value not just for customers but for society.
- I continuously evaluate risks and opportunities.
- I adapt my strategies based on market dynamics.
- I believe strong relationships are the foundation of business success.
- I focus on delivering consistent customer experiences.
- I embrace challenges as opportunities for growth.
- I aim to build a legacy through my entrepreneurial journey.
- I believe discipline and persistence are key traits of successful entrepreneurs.
- I strive to make informed and strategic decisions.
- I believe in lifelong learning and improvement.
- I focus on building a resilient business model.
- I adapt quickly to changing circumstances.
- I maintain a growth mindset in all situations.
- I believe success comes from consistent effort.
- I focus on solving meaningful problems.
- I aim to create innovative solutions.
- I believe strong execution is more important than ideas.
- I continuously push my limits.
- I focus on delivering measurable results.
- I strive for excellence in everything I do.

- I believe in taking ownership of my actions.
- I aim to inspire others through my journey.
- I focus on creating long-term impact.
- I continuously improve my leadership abilities.
- I believe clarity of vision drives success.
- I focus on strategic growth.
- I build systems that scale.
- I optimize performance regularly.
- I strive to stay ahead of industry trends.
- I believe innovation requires courage.
- I focus on disciplined execution.
- I build businesses with purpose.
- I learn from both success and failure.
- I embrace change as a constant.
- I focus on delivering excellence.
- I stay committed to my goals.
- I act with confidence and clarity.
- I build value-driven businesses.
- I believe consistency leads to mastery.
- I strive for continuous growth.
- I focus on meaningful impact.
- I believe persistence always pays off.
- I stay dedicated to my mission.
- I push beyond my comfort zone.
- I stay focused on my vision.
- I act with purpose every day.
- I build something that matters.
- I never stop evolving as an entrepreneur.
- This is a new business idea.

- That product looks good.
- The price is too high.
- The quality is excellent.
- The customer is happy.
- The service is fast.
- The delivery is late.
- The team is ready.
- The work is done.
- The meeting is today.
- The client is waiting.
- The order is confirmed.
- The payment is pending.
- The deal is closed.
- The product is available.
- The stock is limited.
- The demand is high.
- The market is growing.
- The plan is simple.
- The goal is clear.
- Please check the price.
- Please send the details.
- Please confirm the order.
- Please call later.
- Please wait a moment.
- Please share the file.
- Please review this.
- Please sign here.
- Please send payment.
- Please respond quickly.

- Welcome to our business.
- How can we help you?
- What do you need?
- Which product do you want?
- This product is new.
- This one is better.
- That one is cheaper.
- This is high quality.
- That is low cost.
- This is popular.
- The team will handle it.
- The manager will call.
- The staff is working.
- The problem is solved.
- The issue is fixed.
- The report is ready.
- The work is pending.
- The task is assigned.
- The result is good.
- The feedback is positive.
- The product is selling fast.
- The service needs improvement.
- The customer asked questions.
- The team needs support.
- The plan needs changes.
- The budget is small.
- The cost is high.
- The profit is low.
- The idea is interesting.

- The result looks promising.
- The customer is asking for a discount.
- The client wants more details about the product.
- The team is working on the new project.
- The company is planning to expand soon.
- The product is performing well in the market.
- The sales are increasing this month.
- The business is growing steadily.
- The marketing strategy is working effectively.
- The customer feedback is very helpful.
- The service needs some improvement.
- The meeting has been scheduled for tomorrow.
- The team will discuss the new strategy.
- The manager will explain the plan.
- The client has approved the proposal.
- The project has started successfully.
- The results are better than expected.
- The problem has been resolved.
- The issue is being handled carefully.
- The team is focusing on quality.
- The company is aiming for long-term growth.
- The company is improving its customer service.
- The team is developing a new product.
- The business is exploring new markets.
- The company is investing in technology.
- The system is being upgraded.
- The process is becoming more efficient.
- The workflow is well organized.
- The operations are running smoothly.

- The team is meeting deadlines consistently.
- The management is making strategic decisions.
- The customer is satisfied with the service.
- The client is interested in long-term collaboration.
- The customer requested a quick delivery.
- The team responded immediately.
- The issue was resolved professionally.
- The company is focusing on sustainable growth.
- The business is building a strong brand.
- The team is working towards common goals.
- The strategy is designed for long-term success.
- The company is adapting to market changes.
- The company is striving to build a scalable business model.
- The strategy is focused on long-term sustainability.
- The organization is adapting to changing market conditions.
- The leadership team is making data-driven decisions.
- The company is committed to delivering high-quality solutions.
- The business is leveraging technology to improve efficiency.
- The management is focusing on innovation and growth.
- The company is strengthening its market position.
- The team is continuously improving its performance.
- The strategy is aligned with the company's vision.
- Real business speaking style
- The deal looks promising at this stage.
- The proposal needs a few adjustments.
- The client is expecting a detailed explanation.
- The results indicate strong growth potential.
- The company is exploring strategic partnerships.
- The market conditions are becoming more competitive.

- The company is responding proactively to challenges.
- The team is demonstrating strong leadership skills.
- The process has been optimized for better results.
- The organization is focusing on customer satisfaction.
- The company is aiming to expand globally.
- The leadership is driving innovation across departments.
- The strategy emphasizes efficiency and scalability.
- The company is building a strong brand identity.
- The business is creating long-term value.
- The company is balancing profitability with sustainability.
- The organization is committed to ethical business practices.
- The strategy is designed to maximize long-term impact.
- The team is focused on achieving measurable results.
- The business is continuously evolving.
- The company is strengthening customer relationships.
- The leadership is fostering a culture of innovation.
- The strategy is delivering consistent results.
- The organization is maintaining high standards.
- The business is focused on long-term success.
- The company is building a resilient structure.
- The team is aligned with the company's goals.
- The strategy is executed with precision.
- The organization is adapting quickly to change.
- The business is maintaining steady growth.
- The company is focused on delivering excellence.
- The team is committed to continuous improvement.
- The leadership is guiding the company effectively.
- The strategy is producing strong outcomes.
- The organization is driving innovation forward.

- The company is achieving consistent success.
- The business is expanding its reach.
- The team is working collaboratively.
- The strategy is well defined.
- The organization is performing efficiently.
- The company is building a strong future.
- The team is achieving great results.
- The strategy is working effectively.
- The business is growing rapidly.
- The organization is thriving.
- The company is delivering value consistently.
- The team is focused on excellence.
- The strategy is well executed.
- The organization is highly productive.
- The business is scaling successfully.
- The company is reaching new heights.
- The team is exceeding expectations.
- The strategy is creating impact.
- The organization is evolving continuously.
- The business is leading the market.
- The company is setting new standards.
- The team is achieving success together.
- The strategy is driving growth.
- The organization is building a legacy.
- The business is moving forward confidently.
- The company is shaping the future.
- The team is delivering strong performance.
- The strategy is creating opportunities.
- The organization is achieving excellence.

- The business is succeeding globally.
- What do you do?
- Where do you work?
- Where are you working?
- What are you?
- Who do you work for?
- What do you do for living?
- What is you occupation?
- What is you designation?
- What sort of work do you do?
- What's keeping you busy these days?
- How long have you been in your job?
- How long have you been working here?
- Whom do you work for?
- What is your job there?
- What field of work are you in?
- How should I dress?
- What should I wear?
- Good morning, everyone.
- Let's start the meeting.
- Please take your seats.
- Today's agenda is sales growth.
- Can you share the report?
- I will send you an email.
- Please check your inbox.
- The deadline is tomorrow.
- We need to finish this project.
- Let's discuss the budget.
- Can you explain the details?

- Please prepare the presentation.
- We should reduce the cost.
- Our profits are increasing.
- The client is very happy.
- We have a meeting at 10 a.m.
- Please be on time.
- Let's take a short break.
- I agree with your idea.
- That's a good suggestion.
- We need more information.
- Please update the file.
- I will call the customer.
- Can we schedule a meeting?
- Let's fix a new target.
- Please send me the data.
- I will check and confirm.
- Our team is working hard.
- The project is successful.
- We are facing a problem.
- Can you solve this issue?
- Let's find a solution.
- Please share your opinion.
- I will prepare a summary.
- We must complete it today.
- The contract is ready.
- Please sign the agreement.
- The payment is pending.
- Let's finalize the deal.
- The customer is waiting.

- Please answer the call.
- Can you join the meeting?
- I will give a presentation.
- Let's check the figures.
- The report is not clear.
- Please explain once again.
- I understand your concern.
- Let's improve our service.
- We should increase sales.
- This product is in demand.
- Please complete the task.
- Our company is growing.
- We need to hire more staff.
- Training is very important.
- Let's motivate our team.
- Can you prepare the invoice?
- Please check the balance sheet.
- The payment has been received.
- We are waiting for approval.
- Please submit the form.
- I will forward the message.
- Can we change the plan?
- Let's discuss the strategy.
- The client is not satisfied.
- We must improve quality.
- Please note down the points.
- Let's start the project next week.
- Can you manage this work?
- We should meet the deadline.

- Please send the quotation.
- The price is negotiable.
- Let's sign the contract today.
- I will prepare the proposal.
- We need quick action.
- Please update me daily.
- Let's review the progress.
- Our target is very high.
- The manager is not available.
- Please wait in the lobby.
- I will connect you with HR.
- Let's schedule an interview.
- The candidate is qualified.
- Please arrange the documents.
- The printer is not working.
- Call the IT department.
- Please share the password.
- I will join the video call.
- The internet is very slow.
- Can you restart the system?
- Please check the projector.
- Let's start the training session.
- This workshop is useful.
- Please prepare the certificates.
- Our customers are satisfied.
- We must maintain good service.
- Let's celebrate our success.
- Please arrange the meeting room.
- The order has been delivered.

- We are expecting new clients.
- Thank you for your support.
- We have a meeting with the client tomorrow.
- The project deadline is next Monday.
- Our company made a good profit this year.
- Please send me the business report by email.
- Teamwork is very important for success.
- How do you go to office?
- Did you go to office yesterday?
- How much money do you earn for a month?
- We should ask higher salary.
- What work experience do you have?
- I am here to apply for a job.
- I am in IT field.
- I have office tomorrow.
- At what time does the bank close?
- Do you have any vacancy?
- I am unemployed at the moment.
- I had already worked for several years before I got married.
- At what time do you usually go to work?
- This is our main office.
- Do you have another branch?
- Did you hear they hired a new consultant?
- What do you think about the new policies?
- What do you think about the new rules?
- Meet them in person.
- What are your working hours?
- I can't believe how busy we are today.
- I want to work with efficiency.

- I don't delay anything.
- I follow good principles.
- What do you think of the new project?
- How are things at work?
- Any phone call for me?
- Any news?
- Are you interested in that?
- What about your manager?
- Where is the factory?
- How is work going in your department?
- If you are late, again you will be let go.
- Our manager is very strict.
- I am out of work.
- I am a freelance writer.
- I am a new reporter.
- I am looking for a job.
- I am an Entrepreneur.
- I am a Businessman.
- Are you still looking for a job?
- I am not working at the moment.
- I teach English at the high school.
- I work for St.Thomas high school.
- I am into Education.
- I have got a part-time job.
- I agree to your terms.
- We agree to your proposal.
- We will be looking for someone new.
- Can you put through to Vimala in HR please?
- How long have you been working here?

- Have you worked here long?
- Why did you resign the job?
- You have so much experience working in hotels.
- I should have accepted that job offer.
- Because of pressure, I resigned my job.
- I sent my resume to over 10 different companies.
- I work for myself.
- I have my own business.
- I run a retail garment store.
- I am a homemaker.
- I am self-employed.
- I need a job.
- What kind of job do you want?
- He is one of my coworker.
- Did I ask you to resign the job?
- Do you have a full time job?
- Did you get there on time?
- Do you have a part-time job?
- I work as a part timer.
- I have just lost my job.
- You have quit your job, what are you going to do next.
- I have to save my money.
- I am working at two jobs now. I have to make ends meet.
- I hate my job.
- He is still in the office.
- Have you been looking for another job?
- She is currently out of work.
- I am looking for a new job at the moment.
- Is your job stressful?

- I start work at 9 a.m. and get off at 5 p.m.
- I work from 8:00 until 5:00 today.
- I am doing business.
- I work in an office.
- I work at home.
- I am doing the training in IT Company.
- I am training to be an Engineer.
- I am looking for a job.
- He is working in an MNC company.
- He is working as a Teacher in St. John High School.
- He is an Engineer.
- Rahul works in a hospital.
- I am a graduate.
- I am an M.B.A graduate.
- I have done M.C.A.
- I pursued the degree in Business Administration.
- I am sorry. I have no experience.
- I have three years experience in Sales Officer.
- I am an Accountant.
- I am a computer operator.
- I am a nurse.
- I work in a hospital.
- I work for Apollo Hospital.
- I work for HCL.
- I am in charge of a TVS company.
- I am responsible for some workers in that department.
- I have to deal with any complaints.
- I run a restaurant.
- I have to attend conferences.

- I meet clients.
- I advise clients and give them help.
- It involves doing a lot of paperwork.
- It is not easy to find work in big cities.
- I would love to do marketing.
- I work ten-to-six
- I work shift work.
- I am on flexi time.
- I have to work overtime.
- I usually take a break for ten minutes.
- I get some rest.
- I am paid.
- My annual salary is 2 lakh.
- I earn 3000 a week.
- I get holiday pay and sick pay.
- Are you happy with your salary?
- We get a pay raise once a year.
- Can you save any money?
- I can't make ends meet on such a low salary.
- The cost of living is going up too fast.
- The prices go up day to day.
- I am currently staying in a hotel.
- I will be there in couple of hours.
- Do you work in an office?
- The building is on fire.
- I am on the bus.
- He is on the phone right now.
- Call me, I am at home.
- Do you make a lot of money?

- How do you usually pay when you go shopping?
- Is it full-time or part-time?
- Do you have a job?
- What was the last thing you bought?
- Where did you buy it?
- How did you spend it?
- Do you have a credit card?
- Do you have a bank account?
- How often do you use it?
- How do you spend your money?
- How much did you spend yesterday?
- What did you spend it on?
- How do you do it?
- How often do you go shopping?
- Where did you buy it?
- Where would you go to buy books?
- What's your favourite place to shop?
- Do you compare prices at different stores when you go shopping?
- What is the best place to buy home appliances?
- What was the last thing you bought?
- Which do you prefer small local shops or supermarket?
- Do you mind if I take your business card?
- Can we talk a little later?
- Kindly send your response by the end of the day.
- Our company might get the order if the client agrees to the price.
- You should check that document before you send it out.
- How many would like to order?
- How much is the salary?

- How is business going?
- Does the office have Wi-Fi connection?
- Is he bringing the file?
- Is John still working here?
- I overslept this morning and arrived late to the office.
- He has a well paying job.
- He is working here for five years.
- I do social service.
- I am not as experienced as you.
- He needs some career advice.
- Where is Henry transferring to?
- Have you any idea about this product?
- You have got a great personality.
- The manager asked you to wait.
- How long does the company exist?
- Where do you have your bank account?
- I have my account in SBI.
- Ask Thomas to go to the bank.
- Ask him to bring the files.
- I have a meeting tomorrow.
- Have I ever asked you to work on Sundays?
- I don't have time.
- They offered us new project.
- I have been working on that project for the last three weeks.
- It is not worth.
- It is a challenging work for me.
- He is on the other line. (when phone)
- I have a work today.
- Peter has to work today.

- I worked for twelve hours yesterday.
- I can't come to work today. I am ill.
- I am very tired because I have been working all day.
- Sir, Sam is on leave today.
- How long is he on leave?
- No problem.
- I have no objection.
- Can you complete the work in three days?
- I want to leave the job for better prospects.
- I manage quality control.
- He is the supervisor.
- When will you be back?
- This is a deal.
- I will be right back.
- I will be there as we have agreed.
- Can they provide hospitality?
- Take your time.
- She is not here at the moment.
- I am here to see Mr:Anand.
- I have an appointment with Mr.Sam.
- Someone called Tom wanted to talk to you.
- Could you please tell Mr.Austin, I am here?
- Here is my visiting card.
- What are you going to say?
- Can I do the job?
- Sales have been dull compare to last year.
- Could I have time to consider your offer?
- May I come over tomorrow?
- We need to discuss some important matter.

- I worked there for five years.
- Feel free to call me if you have any doubt.
- Sorry to keep you waiting.
- Will you be available on Monday morning?
- Where is the warehouse?
- Where is the godown?
- How to maintain the stocks?
- How many people are working here?
- When is the good time for you?
- Please come over this evening.
- What time should I be there?
- In which department is Maya working?
- Is the office fully computerized?
- Stop telling what to do and mind your business.
- Are you trying to make me a fool?
- Could you send me the report, please?
- Don’t tell me that. You have to send the report immediately.
- Please call this number if you require any further information.
- Could you give me a minute, please?
- When is the deadline?
- I have to make the deadline.
- I have to make the decision.
- I am looking forward to do business with you.
- Any mails for me?
- When does the meeting start?
- The manager has postponed the meeting.
- The meeting was cancelled.
- The meeting will start on time.
- Let me know when you are available.

- I am in low spirits today.
- I am not sure that is a good idea.
- I am not satisfied with you work.
- Sir, I think you might be mistaken.
- I am not quite satisfied with this work.
- He regretted his mistake.
- Totally my fault.
- I am confused whether to accept this deal.
- I really need your suggestion.
- This is the best thing to do.
- I was nervous to initiate a conversation with my boss.
- That's interesting! How did you get involved with that?
- The manager seems to be in a good mood today.
- Has John arrived yet?
- Everyone is friendly.
- What is this job about?
- I love my job. I help people become fluent in English.
- The work is not finished yet.
- He is over working.
- I refused the offer.
- Could I come over?
- I heard that your branch office will be moving to a new building.
- What is his role in this project?
- Who is in charge of this project?
- The project cost us 1crore.
- His mistake cost us 10 lakhs.
- I take responsibility for my mistake.
- Do you know anyone here?
- What time does the office close?

- I am fed up with my job. I need a change.
- I can lose my job. It is so stressful.
- I cannot bear working on Sundays.
- Sorry, it didn't work out.
- Any different ideas?
- I would like to open a current account.
- I am a sales officer of the company.
- This is our sales manager, Mr. Charles.
- We do both import and export business.
- We employ 200 people in company.
- I want to talk to your manager.
- Do you have an appointment, please?
- I have an appointment at 11a.m.
- May I know what company you are from?
- What is your business scope?
- Our business scope includes stationary items, clothes and cosmetics.
- Our products are greatly appreciated by people.
- Our products are superior in quality.
- Our products are mainly engaged in electrical appliance.
- If the prices are reasonable, we are ready to become your agent.
- We will give you a reply as soon as possible.
- We will send you a list.
- I cannot meet your demand.
- Will you consider our proposal?
- What is the monthly turnover of your company?
- We offer you advertising support and spare parts service.
- I put advertisement in the newspaper.
- We will make efforts to push your products.

- That's why we come here.
- May I know what type of products you are making?
- It will take 5-6 days to process.
- How much is your servicing charge?
- We will supply you the material on time.
- Well, we agree to that.
- You should send replacements in time.
- We need those items urgently.
- It is the rules of the company.
- My offer is based on reasonable profit.
- Can't you reduce your price anymore?
- Sorry, we cannot.
- Your price is higher than other showroom.
- We have better quality products.
- The quality of products is guaranteed.
- Here is a catalog. Take a look.
- You can have a look at the catalog.
- It's a reasonable price.
- Your prices are good.
- We cannot accept your offer unless the price is reduced.
- Hope we can get your order soon.
- That is why we prefer to order from your company.
- I will try to buy in a bulk.
- I would like to have your quotation.
- Thank you very much for the order.
- Thank you for your inquiry.
- Here are our dealer price lists.
- I can do that for you as well.
- This is our final rate.

- You have to pay interest every month.
- We know that.
- We agree.
- The business is good for both of us.
- What do you think about it?
- I don’t know what you mean.
- How many models/products do you want?
- How long will you keep the offers open?
- Let me see on Friday.
- Looking forward to your reply.
- I look forward to your settlement at an early date.
- Please tell me your requirements.
- I would like to hear your requirements about the product.
- We assure you that the product will be made before June.
- What’s wrong with the goods?
- It has lots of damage.
- How many of them are damaged?
- You have to re-check the product.
- We found a small damage in the product.
- We will give you a reply tomorrow.
- This kind of incident has never occurred before.
- Let me see… it seems like we had a mistake on delivery.
- How will you deal with this matter?
- I am looking forward to having your early reply to this matter.
- Please give us some time, we should inquire into that matter.
- I do apologize for that.
- Ok, reply to me as soon as possible, please.
- The expenses amounted to 20 lakhs.
- We will compensate.

- I hope this incident will not bring any harm to our business.
- I hope so. Be careful next time.
- Don't worry. I will make it.
- I don't know who to talk to.
- I don't know what you want.
- I would like negotiate with your manager.
- I hope you will seriously consider our claim.
- I hope this matter will not affect our business.
- I hope this business will bring benefit to both of us.
- Can you tell the reason for damage?
- When is the deadline for registration?
- Has the registration begun?
- Can you tell me the registration process?
- The deadline is on Wednesday.
- Can I book it for tomorrow morning?
- Do we need to pay the deposit?
- Yes, you need to pay 20%.
- Can I transfer money by mobile phone?
- If you need any help, please let me know.
- Show me the model, please.
- Let me take you there.
- They look nice.
- We will send you the order very soon.
- The prices are reasonable you can ask anywhere.
- I find that your prices are too high.
- Anything I can do for you?
- I am looking forward to cooperate with you next time.
- The price varies according to the model.

- Our customers complain that the products are much inferior in quality.
- Compare with other brands, we have good quality.
- Would you tell us the model you want?
- We require immediate payment.
- I am looking forward to meeting you.
- I am looking forward to hearing from you.
- I hope we can do business together.
- I hope we can cooperate.
- I hope we can continue our business.
- I think that this market trend will continue.
- I hope that the matter can be brought to a satisfactory solution.
- Sorry, we cannot make any discounts.
- We invite quotation of the lowest price.
- We agree on the contract.
- We agree the price.
- We will pay in cash in 5 days.
- Tell about your payment terms.
- The price is a little higher than the market price.
- Our price is the most favorable.
- What is the fixed price for this product?
- If you are interested, we will offer as soon as possible.
- We order 500 books now.
- The product is demand in this area.
- This model is demand in our country.
- Thank you for your interest in our company.
- The stock market opens at 9:15 a.m.
- The market closes at 3:30 p.m.
- I want to buy some shares.

- I want to sell my shares.
- What is the price of this share today?
- The share price is going up.
- The share price is going down.
- The market is bullish today.
- The market is bearish today.
- I invested in Reliance shares.
- He lost money in intraday trading.
- She made a profit in short-term trading.
- This company has declared a dividend.
- My portfolio is growing.
- I want to diversify my investments.
- The Sensex is rising today.
- The Nifty is falling today.
- The market is very volatile.
- I will buy more shares if the price drops.
- He sold his shares at a high price.
- She bought the shares at a low price.
- I am holding my shares for the long term.
- He is a long-term investor.
- She is a short-term trader.
- The company launched its IPO last week.
- The IPO was oversubscribed.
- I applied for the IPO.
- My shares were allotted.
- I did not get the allotment.
- The company's market value is very high.
- The company's market value is low.
- He checks the stock price every day.

- She follows the market news daily.
- The market sentiment is positive.
- The market sentiment is negative.
- The broker helps me to trade.
- I placed a buy order.
- I placed a sell order.
- The order was executed.
- The order is still pending.
- The share is at its highest price.
- The share is at its lowest price.
- He booked his profit.
- She booked her loss.
- I use a trading app on my phone.
- The app shows live prices.
- The internet is slow, trading is difficult.
- Please update your KYC.
- The account is activated.
- The account is suspended.
- The company announced quarterly results.
- The results are very good.
- The results are not good.
- The share price increased after results.
- The share price fell after results.
- The government announced a new policy.
- The policy affects the stock market.
- Foreign investors are buying shares.
- Domestic investors are selling shares.
- The trading volume is high today.
- The trading volume is low today.

- The share has given good returns.
- The share has given poor returns.
- He is analyzing the charts.
- She studies technical analysis.
- He studies fundamental analysis.
- The support level is strong.
- The resistance level is weak.
- The market trend is upward.
- The market trend is downward.
- I am a beginner in stock trading.
- He is an experienced trader.
- She is a professional investor.
- The mutual fund invests in shares.
- SIP is a safe way to invest.
- The stock market has risks.
- Higher risk gives higher return.
- Lower risk gives lower return.
- I prefer safe investments.
- He likes risky investments.
- Gold price affects the stock market.
- Crude oil price affects the market.
- Inflation affects investments.
- Interest rate hike affects shares.
- The company announced a bonus issue.
- The company announced a stock split.
- The company announced a buyback.
- The shareholders approved the decision.
- The company has strong growth.
- The company has weak growth.

- The share is undervalued.
- The share is overvalued.
- The market crashed suddenly.
- The market recovered quickly.
- The investor is confident.
- The investor is worried.
- I will hold my shares.
- I will sell my shares tomorrow.
- I will buy more if the price falls.
- The stock market is full of opportunities.
- I bought 50 shares of TCS yesterday.
- The stock market is very volatile today.
- Infosys announced a good dividend.
- The Sensex is going up.
- The market is bearish this week.
- He made a profit in intraday trading.
- I want to diversify my portfolio.
- The company launched its IPO last month.
- She suffered a huge loss in the share market.
- Long-term investors usually get good returns.
- Thank you for visiting our bank.
- Is there anything else I can help you with?
- Would you like to open an account?
- Do you want a savings account or a current account?
- Please fill in this application form.
- May I have your ID proof?
- Please provide your address proof.
- Kindly attach a passport-size photograph.
- Your account will be activated within two days.

- Here is your account number.
- Please set your signature specimen here.
- Do you want to link your mobile number with this account?
- How much would you like to deposit?
- Please fill in the deposit slip.
- Kindly sign here.
- Do you want the receipt?
- Please count the cash before leaving.
- Your deposit has been successful.
- This is your stamped receipt.
- Would you like to deposit by cheque or cash?
- Please write your account number clearly.
- Thank you for your deposit.
- How much would you like to withdraw?
- Please fill in the withdrawal slip.
- Kindly sign in the space provided.
- Please show me your passbook.
- Would you like the amount in cash or draft?
- Kindly verify the cash.
- Here is your money.
- Please check the amount carefully.
- Withdrawal has been processed.
- Thank you for using our services.
- Would you like to deposit this cheque?
- Please endorse the cheque at the back.
- The cheque needs verification.
- This cheque will be cleared in two working days.
- Kindly write the payee's name clearly.
- This cheque has insufficient funds.

- Please issue a fresh cheque.
- Would you like to request a cheque book?
- Please collect your cheque book at the counter.
- The cheque has been returned unpaid.
- Do you want to apply for a debit card?
- Please fill out this ATM card form.
- Your card will be delivered within 7 working days.
- Kindly enter your PIN carefully.
- Do not share your PIN with anyone.
- Would you like to change your PIN?
- Your card has been blocked successfully.
- Please wait while I generate a new card.
- You can withdraw cash from any ATM.
- Thank you for using your debit card.
- Are you interested in applying for a loan?
- Do you want a personal loan or a home loan?
- Please submit your income proof.
- Kindly provide your salary slip.
- We also need your bank statement.
- The loan process will take 3 to 5 working days.
- Your loan has been approved.
- Please sign the loan agreement.
- This is your repayment schedule.
- Kindly pay your EMI on time.
- Would you like to activate net banking?
- Please fill out this net banking request form.
- Here is your user ID and password.
- Please change your password immediately.
- Do not share your login details.

- You can transfer funds online.
- Would you like to enable mobile banking?
- Kindly download our banking app.
- All your transactions will be secure.
- Thank you for using online banking.
- How may I assist you today?
- Could you please repeat that?
- I will check and update you.
- Please wait for a moment.
- I am sorry, this service is not available.
- May I have your account number?
- Please confirm your mobile number.
- Do you want to update your address?
- Kindly sign here for verification.
- Your request has been recorded.
- Your account has been closed.
- Please collect your final statement.
- Kindly return your unused cheque leaves.
- Thank you for banking with us.
- We appreciate your trust.
- Please let us know if you face any issues.
- This is your acknowledgment receipt.
- Kindly give us your feedback.
- We value your relationship with our bank.
- Have a wonderful day ahead!
- I am looking to buy a house.
- Do you have any properties for sale?
- How much does this house cost?
- Is the price negotiable?

- What is the total area of the property?
- How old is the building?
- Does this house have a clear title?
- Can I see the property documents?
- Is this property approved by the bank?
- Does the house face east or west?
- What is the registration fee?
- How much is the property tax?
- Can I take a loan for this property?
- When can I move in?
- Are there any hidden charges?
- Can I meet the owner directly?
- What is the resale value of this property?
- Is this a ready-to-move house?
- Does this apartment come with furniture?
- Is this a gated community?
- I am looking for a flat for rent.
- What is the monthly rent?
- How much is the security deposit?
- Is electricity included in the rent?
- Do I need to sign an agreement?
- How long is the lease period?
- Is the rent negotiable?
- Are pets allowed here?
- Is there 24-hour water supply?
- Does this flat have power backup?
- How far is the bus stop from here?
- Is there a lift in this building?
- Can I sublet the house?

- How much is the maintenance charge?
- Is parking included in the rent?
- How many people can stay here?
- When is the rent due every month?
- Do I have to paint the house before leaving?
- Is the flat semi-furnished or fully furnished?
- Can I extend the rental agreement?
- I want to sell my property.
- How much is the market value now?
- Can you find a buyer for me?
- What commission do you charge?
- How long will it take to sell?
- Should I advertise the property?
- Do I need to renovate before selling?
- Can you arrange site visits for buyers?
- What documents are required for selling?
- Should I register the property in advance?
- Can I get an advance payment?
- Is the buyer ready to pay in cash?
- Can you list my property online?
- How much profit can I expect?
- Do I need to pay capital gains tax?
- What is the current demand in this area?
- Will you help with legal paperwork?
- Can I sell it through auction?
- How do I transfer ownership?
- Will you handle negotiations?
- Does this house have a garden?
- Is there a swimming pool?

- How many bedrooms are there?
- Does the flat have a balcony?
- Is there a modular kitchen?
- Is this house furnished?
- Does the property have CCTV?
- Is the neighborhood safe?
- Are there supermarkets nearby?
- How far is the nearest school?
- Does this area have good water supply?
- Is there a hospital nearby?
- How far is the railway station?
- Does this property have internet connection?
- Is there a children's play area?
- Does this flat get enough sunlight?
- What floor is this apartment on?
- Does the house have a guest room?
- Is there a separate servant room?
- How many parking slots are available?
- I am interested in this property.
- Can we fix an appointment for site visit?
- What are the nearby landmarks?
- Is this property under litigation?
- Do you provide loan assistance?
- Can you recommend a good lawyer?
- I want to invest in land.
- What is the guideline value here?
- Can I buy property in installments?
- Do I need a guarantor for the loan?
- Is this a freehold or leasehold property?

- Can I construct an additional floor?
- Does this plot have proper boundaries?
- Can I get an estimate for construction?
- What is the return on investment?
- Are there any upcoming projects nearby?
- Is the area developing fast?
- Can you help me with registration?
- What are the payment terms?
- Thank you for your assistance.
- We need to sign the agreement today.
- Please read the contract carefully before signing.
- The lawyer will explain the legal terms.
- This document is legally binding.
- We must follow all company policies.
- The deal will be valid for one year.
- You have the right to cancel the contract.
- The payment terms are clearly mentioned.
- We need legal approval before starting.
- The agreement protects both parties.
- Please submit the required legal documents.
- The lawyer will draft the contract.
- We should register the company legally.
- The terms and conditions are attached.
- The client must follow the agreement rules.
- This issue will go to legal notice.
- The company is responsible for compliance.
- The contract starts from next month.
- The lawyer will check the documents.
- Please keep a copy of the agreement.

- The agreement must be signed by both parties.
- We need to renew the contract next year.
- The lawyer will guide us on legal matters.
- This case may go to arbitration.
- We should settle the dispute legally.
- The contract includes confidentiality terms.
- We must follow government regulations.
- The company is liable for damages.
- The lawyer will file the legal notice.
- The agreement cannot be changed without consent.
- Please verify the signature on the document.
- The contract is valid under the law.
- The agreement mentions the penalty clause.
- All disputes will be solved in court.
- We must keep all records legally safe.
- The lawyer will explain our legal rights.
- The contract has a clear start and end date.
- The client agreed to the legal terms.
- Please make two copies of the contract.
- The company must pay as per agreement.

9. DISCOUNT / CONCESSION

- We will give some discount.
- How much is the maximum or minimum discount?
- Our maximum is 15%, and minimum is 10%.
- We will reduce the price by 5% percent.
- I am afraid I can't accept 5%.
- I would suggest another three percent.
- If we order 500 units, what will be your offer?

- How much discount could you offer?
- We have the offer ready for you.
- If you double the order, we will give you 10% discount.
- If you order more than 500, we will give you 5% commission.
- 5% is too low, we want at least 10% concession.
- The reduction is at least 5%.
- I expect that you will offer us a lower price.
- A 5% commission is too low for us.
- You have to give some 10% concession in commission.
- If you give me a 5% reduction, I will order….
- We ask you to discount by 15% off the list price.
- It is valid within ten days.
- You will get a discount if you pay today.

10. PRODUCT DELIVERY

- The time of delivery is very important to us.
- Delivery would be a week from the date of ordering.
- Can you make the delivery before the weekend?
- I can assure you we will deliver it to you on time.
- We will inform you before the delivery.
- It will take time to deliver.
- I am calling to tell you that we have not yet received the product.
- Do you know the date of delivery?
- We will send them in this week.
- You should not fail to deliver in time.
- Your delay in delivery has caused problems on both our customer and us.
- Take it easy, we promise you to make delivery on time.

- You can expect delivery in one week.
- If you are unable to deliver within two days, we shall be cancelled our order.
- That won't happen. You are surely receiving it within two days.
- Haven't you received the product?
- We have received the product.
- It will dispatch soon.

11. SALES INCREASE / DECREASE

- There has been a slow increase in sales this month.
- Sales have been increase steadily.
- Our sales are going up this year.
- It increases steadily.
- Our sales are climbing.
- The turnover will be increased.
- Our profits increased by 100% this year.
- Our profits have sky rocketed.
- Our sales are losing.
- The profits of the company are going down.
- Our profits are decreasing / falling.
- Sales are starting to fall.
- There is a gradual climb in sales.
- The company has a steady climb in profits.
- Our company is experiencing massive gains.

12. APPRECIATING WORKERS

- You have done a great job!
- You are doing a good job.
- You are a genius.

- You are getting better every day.
- You are very good at that.
- He is the best in the business.
- Keep working, you are getting better.
- I am happy to see you working like that.
- Keep up the good work.
- I admire your work.
- Don't worry nobody is perfect first time.

13. SHOPPING

- May I help you?
- How can I help you?
- What are you looking for?
- Can I help you?
- I need a shirt.
- What do you want sir?
- Do you want to buy anything?
- I am just looking.
- I am just browsing.
- I am looking for a formal shirt.
- I am looking for a black shirt.
- Do you sell jeans?
- Can you help me with this?
- It is on the first floor.
- Have look at this one.
- How much is this?
- It is too loose/long.
- It is too big/small.
- It is too tight.

- Do you have a pant to match this shirt?
- These jeans are too loose.
- Can I try this on?
- Is it wrinkle-free?
- This clothe is wrinkle resistant, it resists liquid spills and food stains.
- Where can I find shirt?
- Do you have jeans pant?
- These jeans are too tight.
- Do have it in medium size?
- Do you have alteration service?
- Do you have T-shirt?
- It looks a little bit big.
- Come on, try on these jeans. They will look great.
- What else is new?
- Is this on sale?
- I bought this saree in Boutique.
- What else is available?
- I don't want any of that.
- Where is men's wear?
- Where is the children's section?
- Let me try it on and see how it fits.
- Please, try this shirt.
- Can I try it on?
- Are these new clothes?
- May I try this shirt on?
- Choose whatever you want.
- Do you have this in red?
- I will take it.

- Shall I bring you another pair of shoes?
- Do you think this colour suits me?
- Is this what you wanted?
- How much is the shirt for?
- Do you have a smaller/bigger size?
- Do you have it in larger size?
- When will the new collection arrive?
- Is this what you were looking for?
- What size do you want?
- The blue one is too bright for me.
- It fits you perfectly.
- That's nice.
- It's a factory outlet. So the price is cheap.
- Try this saree.
- Turn around, wow! That looks great on you.
- Look at yourself in the mirror.
- That looks great.
- I don't like this design.
- I bought this in retail store.
- It will be very fine for you.
- You have a good taste of clothes.
- Is this free?
- I like this one.
- Do you have it in another colour?
- What colour do you want madam?
- This dress also comes in blue, green violet and red.
- Just show me. I will choose.
- Try this shoe.
- Anything new?

- Kids section is in the third floor.
- The price is cheaper too.
- It is too much.
- Excuse me, where is the trial room?
- Where is the changing room?
- Excuse me, do you work here?
- Could you help me to try it on?
- Do you have any new model?
- How is this part?
- Can you show me that one?
- I cannot see the price tag.
- How much is it for?
- Is there any discount?
- Can you gift wrap that?
- I saw lower price at other shops.
- I am giving it to you for nothing.
- Where is the billing counter?
- I am paying in cash.
- Where can I pay?
- Sorry I don't have cash.
- Sorry, I don't have a change.
- What is the cost of the cabbage?
- Where will I find vegetables?
- Can you tell me where I can find cool drinks?
- When do you close the shop?
- Are you open on Sunday?
- When are you open the shop?
- I like your dressing sense.
- You are so charming.

- Let me see how you look in this churidar.
- You look great in this dress.
- You are always a centre of attention.
- I love the way you carry yourself.
- You have an amazing personality.
- Would you like anything else?
- Sorry, we don't have any stock left in that colour.
- I would like to return/exchange this?
- Can I exchange it?
- What time do you open the shop?
- Is there any discount on this?
- It costs too much.
- It is costly.
- It is a good price.
- We have a special offer for this one: buy one and get one free.
- Do you think it is too expensive?
- It costs a fortune.
- I don't have enough money to buy it.
- It was a real bargain.
- It was dirt cheap.
- That is exorbitant.
- That's very expensive.
- That's a bit pricey.
- That is a bit steep.
- It is 20% off.
- I can give you 10 percent discount.
- The changing room is over there.
- It is a fair price shop.
- Prices vary widely from shop to shop.

- How much do I have to pay after discount?
- Do you accept credit card?
- Can I pay with my credit card?
- Please enter your pin.
- Please wait for one moment.
- Sign here, please.
- Can I get a receipt?
- Of course, here you go.
- The cost of the car is 5 lakhs.
- This car costs 8 lakhs.
- Thank you for shopping with us!
- It cost an arm and a leg.
- That's a daylight robbery.
- You spend money like water.
- You are spending lavishly.
- Is there anything you can do about the price?
- I am a regular customer here. Please offer me a better price.
- Isn't too expensive how about Rs. 450/-
- How about this one?
- Can you lower the price?
- The cost is too much.
- What if I buy in bulk?
- I think I might be able to find it at a better price.
- Isn't there a discount on this?
- It is too expensive.
- Is that the best price you can give me?

PAY

- Can we have the bill, please?

- Do you accept credit cards?
- Could I have the check/bill please?
- Do you have a change?
- Can we have separate bill/check?
- Can I get the bill, please?
- Could you bring me the bill, please?
- Could we have the check, please?
- Can I have the check, please?
- We'll take the check.
- We are going to split the bill.
- There seems to be a mistake in the bill.
- How would you like to pay, cash or by credit card?
- Do you accept credit card?
- Here 500 rupees. You can keep the change.
- Is the service included in the bill?

14. HOTEL

- Do you have a reservation?
- We have executive suite.
- We have royal suite (luxurious house in a hotel).
- This hotel has different Amenities
  (spa, gym, pool and theatre etc.)
- May I have your name, please?
- Would you tell me your name?
- Your good name, please?
- How do you spell your name, please?
- How long will you be staying?
- How many guests are with you?
- Could you please fill out this form?

- Please sign your name here.
- May I see your I.D., please?
- Do you need help with your bags?
- Do you need a wake-up call?
- Hello, Marriott Hotel, how may I help you? (at phone)
- Is there anything else we can help you with?
- I am sorry, we don't have any rooms
- Your room is on the third floor.
- Would you like smoking or non-smoking?
- You can take lift.
- We have Wi-Fi.
- If you have a laptop, you can use the internet for free.
- Here is your room key.
- For what date do you want reservation?
- How many days will you be staying?
- Do you need a single room or a double room?
- How many days do you want to stay?
- How will you be paying Mr. John?
- Would you like king size bed or two double beds?
- I have allotted room number 301 to you, Sir.
- Shall I help you with your luggage?
- Room boy will take you to your room.
- You have free Wi-Fi in your room.
- You have to pay advance.
- This is a no-smoking place.
- Sorry, pets are not allowed.
- Your room number is 302.
- Here is your key.
- We have room service you can order food to your room service.

- Housekeeping will clean your room.
- There is a restaurant on the ground floor.
- Breakfast is served at the hotel restaurant from6 to 10 am.
- Bed sheets and towels are available at the front desk.
- You have to pay an extra fee for a late check-out.
- Check-out time is 11:00 in the morning.
- Will you be staying for some more days?
- Thank you for staying with us.
- Enjoy your stay here.

CUSTOMER

- Excuse me, I need a room to stay.
- Is there a room available in this hotel?
- How much is it per night in this hotel?
- I am going to stay here for a month.
- I would like a room, please. What is the room rate?
- I would like a room with a balcony.
- Do you have a conference room?
- Do I have to make a reservation?
- I would like to make reservation.
- I have a reservation in the name of Joseph.
- I would like to check-in right now.
- Hello, is it hotel Marriott?
- What are the charges for a single bed room?
- Do I have to pay any advance?
- Do I have to pay an extra charge?
- How many stars does the hotel have?
- Is breakfast included?
- Is the tax included?

- A single room is enough for me.
- Does the room have internet connection?
- What is the room number?
- I would like to reserve a room for two nights.
- I would like to cancel my reservation.
- I would like to book a room, please.
- I would like a single room, please.
- Do you provide a pickup service?
- I would like a double room, please.
- Do you have any rooms available for… (the seventh of May)
- Does the room have air-conditioning?
- Is there a spa in your hotel?
- Does your hotel have meeting hall?
- I left the key in my room.
- When can I check-in?
- Can I see the room, please?
- Can someone help me with my bags?
- Could I have a wake-up call at six o'clock please?
- When is check-out time?
- Could we please check-out a little later?
- Could you please wake me up by 5 o'clock in the morning?
- The room is too noisy.
- I would like to change my room.
- We need housekeeping service, please.
- We would like to stay for an extra day.
- I would like to stay a little longer, please.
- I have lost my room key.
- What time is checkout?
- We are checking out now.

- Is there another exit?
- We really enjoyed our stay.

15. COMPLAINT & ACCEPTANCE

- I want to complain about your service.
- I am sorry to say this but it is the fact.
- I am angry about your attitude.
- Look, I am sorry to trouble you, but…
- I am writing to complain about the food.
- I am writing this letter to indicate the problem that I encounter in your hotel.
- Sorry to bother you but…
- I am afraid I have got a complaint about your product.
- I am really sorry, but this will never happen again.
- I wish it would never happen.
- I am sorry, we will do our best.
- We promise never to do the same mistake again.
- Oh, I am really sorry for that mistake.

16. RESTAURANT

WAITER / WAITRESS

- May I help you?
- What can I do for you?
- Can I help you?
- Do you have a reservation?
- Have you booked a table?
- A table for how many?
- How many of you?
- I will show you to your table.

- There will be a table for you in ten minutes.
- We are fully booked at the moment, could you come back a bit later?
- Would you like to wait in the bar?
- If you wait, there'll be a table for you free in a minute.
- Smoking or non-smoking?
- Of course, please come this way.
- Do you need a booster seat for the child?
- Your table isn't quite ready yet.
- Please come this way.
- Would you follow me, please?
- I am sorry, there are no tables available.
- Sorry, no pets are allowed.
- Sorry, smoking is not allowed.
- Here's the menu.
- Are you ready to order?
- Can I get you anything to drink?
- How many would you like?
- Would you like to have any soup item before the main course, Sir?
- Would like a starter?
- Any side dish, Sir?
- Would you like anything to drink?
- What would you like to start with?
- Would you like sugar and milk?
- How much sugar would you like?
- What would you like for your main course?
- Would you like dessert?
- Would you like an appetizer?

- Would you like coffee or tea?
- Do you want some more coffee?
- Do you want anything else?
- Would you like it hot or cold?
- Would you like something to eat?
- Would you like anything else?
- Would you like grilled chicken?
- What side dish would you like?
- Would you like to try?
- What do you like to eat for breakfast?
- We have got some fresh chicken.
- Today's special is garlic fish.
- I'm sorry, we are out of fish.
- Can I get you anything else?
- Let me repeat your order.
- Here is your coffee.
- Here your water.
- Would you like something to drink?
- Would you like another drink?
- Would you like some more tea?
- There is one left.
- Any juice or fruit salad?
- Was everything alright with your meal?
- Today we have fruit salad.
- Would you like to order a drink now?
- Enjoy your meal.
- Have some more.
- Please take some more food.
- Would you like some more of this?

- Hot or iced?
- What kind of ice cream do you want?
- We have chocolate, vanilla and strawberry.
- I'm sorry, we don't accept credit cards.
- Would you like to pay together or separate?
- The total for your lunch is 1200 rupees.
- That would be 450 rupees.
- Let me change it for you.
- Let me take it back for you.
- I am sorry that I misheard you.
- I am very sorry, sir!
- I am so sorry, I'll change it for you straight away.
- I am sorry, but the prawn is finished.
- I am sorry, I will get you a new order.
- Sorry, the chickens are off.
- I don't think we have anymore fish left.
- I will check in the kitchen.
- The restaurant is closing in ten minutes.
- Thank you sir, we hope you enjoyed the dinner.
- Thank you, please come again.
- Thanks for visiting.
- Please come again.

CUSTOMER

- Are you open?
- Is this seat taken?
- I would like to have a table for three people.
- I have a reservation in the name of Michael.
- A table for two please.

- I booked a table for two people.
- It is under the name of Andy.
- May we sit at this table?
- I booked a table for two at 7p.m.
- A table for two please.
- We have a reservation.
- May we sit at this table?
- Would you follow me, please?
- Excuse me, waiter.
- There are four of us.
- We have been sitting here for almost 15 minutes.
- The menu, please.
- Could we have a menu, please?
- Could you bring us the menu, please?
- May I see the menu, please?
- Can I see the desert menu please?
- What is today's special?
- What is to eat?
- Can we change our table?
- Can we have a table for two, please?
- What is for lunch?
- I have coffee, please.
- I like my coffee black.
- Three coffee, please.
- One black coffee.
- What is for dessert?
- I have fresh orange juice, please.
- Do you have any fresh fruit?
- Do you have roasted fish?

- Waiter! Three plate Biriyani.
- Waiter! Bring two plates of Biriyani.
- First bring me a Dosa for the child.
- Bring two pieces on that.
- I would like a bowl of mutton soup, please.
- I would like a grilled chicken for the main course.
- What do you recommend for breakfast?
- What do you like to have for breakfast?
- No, thanks I am full after the meal.
- That'll be all for now.
- Fruit salad and that's all.
- That's all, thank you.
- May I have a fork/spoon?
- My favorite food here is chicken tikka.
- I have many favourite foods.
- Which is one of them?
- What does it taste like?
- Would/could you pass the salt please?
- Can you please pass the salt?
- Could you bring us the salt/pepper/ketchup please?
- I will have a soup as a starter.
- I will have the mutton Biriyani for the main course.
- I would like some mineral water with a lemon, please.
- Just some tap water, please?
- Do you have a wine list?
- Can you recommend an appetizer?
- May I have some water, please?
- May I get a glass of hot water?
- I would like to have a Mutton Dosa.

- I will have Vegetable Biriyani.
- I'd like mutton Biriyani and ice-cream, please.
- I will have a chicken omelet.
- Do you have Barbeque Chicken?
- Do you have any specials? I will take that.
- Is there anything to eat?
- What do you recommend? (to waiter)
- Could we also have some garlic bread?
- Please make this soup 1 by 2.
- Please see to it, that the food is non-spicy, non-greasy (oily).
- I would like to order my food now.
- May I get an order of barbeque wings?
- Could I have the chicken wing please?
- Is the Salmon steamed or fried?
- I would like a lemon juice.
- We would like to order three chicken Biriyani and some fish fries.
- We'll have the soup and the chicken Biriyani.
- What kind of ice cream do you have?
- Just some water, please.
- Could you give me some salt?
- Let's have 3 coffees, please.
- A cup of coffee please.
- I feel thirsty. Shall we have some lemon juice?
- Does this contain sea food?
- I would like a slice of pizza, please.
- We would like 2 coffees and 2 teas.
- Would you bring me some coffee?
- Could I have some milk please?

- The coffee is hot enough to drink.
- The coffee is cold.
- The coffee is very hot but I can drink it.
- The coffee is too hot to drink.
- We'd like a little longer, please.
- We need a few more minutes before we order.
- We are ready to order.
- I would like a salad.
- We need another fork.
- There is a fly in my soup.
- We would like to see the desert menu, please.
- Can I change my order please?
- I'm sorry, but this is cold.
- Excuse me, but I didn't order this.
- I'm sorry, but can I change my order?
- I am afraid, I didn't order this.
- I am sorry, but I think I ordered Dosa.
- Could I have a doggy bag? (left over get parcel)

FEED BACK

- This food is very tasty.
- It's delicious.
- That was a good breakfast.
- Everything tastes great.
- These sweets are very tasty.
- I am really enjoying this.
- These sweets are absolutely scrumptious.
- That cake looks very tempting.
- That cake looks absolutely irresistible.

- This food is fresh.
- The food is great.
- The food was very unpleasant.
- The food was absolutely disgusting.
- This bread is stale.
- The broth is cold and delightful.
- This fish is raw.
- The meat is not cooked well.
- The food was bad.
- This ice-cream is solid.
- This soup is very thick / very runny.
- The food is cold.
- It doesn't taste right.
- It tasted astringent due to overcooking.
- It was rotten.
- It smelt like a decomposing carcass.
- It is savorless (insipid, flavorless).
- It caused severe nausea.
- The chicken was not properly cooked.
- The food was not hygienic
- Minuscule hair strands were found in the meals.

17. DESCRIBING TASTE

- It is delicious. (pleasant taste)
- It was awful. (very bad)
- It is sweet. (Full of sugar or honey)
- The food was tasty. (good flavor)
- It is piquant.(pleasantly spicy taste)
- It is salt.(full of salt)

- It is sour / tart.(acid taste, like lime or vinegar)
- It is bitter.(strong, sharp taste)
- The food was spicy / hot. (burning taste, because of strong spices)
- It is tangy. (taste that stings your tongue)
- It is mild. (not having a strong taste)
- It was bland.(not having an interesting taste)
- It's disgusting.(very bad taste)
- It is juicy. (contain lot of juice)
- It is stale.(not fresh)
- It is greasy/oily.(food that has fried in oil)
- It was mushy. (food that is very soft)
- It was succulent. (juicy, moist)
- It's yummy. (delicious)
- It's appealing. (tempting)
- It's mouthwatering.(delicious)
- It's harsh.(unpleasant taste)
- It was tasteless. (lacking flavor)
- It is hot. (plenty of chilly)
- It was salty.(full of salt)

RESTROOM

- Is there a bathroom here?
- Where is the toilet?
- Where is the restroom?
- Where is the bathroom?
- Is there a restroom here?
- Is there a toilet here?
- Is there a ladies room nearby?

- Is there a men's room nearby?
- How can I find a toilet?
- There is a public toilet close to here.

18. ASKING & GIVING DIRECTION

- Excuse me, do you know where the post office?
- Excuse me, how can I go to the temple?
- Excuse me, where is the church here?
- Do you know where the Royal Court building is?
- Excuse me, is there a hotel near here?
- Excuse me, could you tell me the way to the hotel?
- Excuse me, do you know where the stadium is?
- Could you tell me if there is a police station near here?
- Where is the town hall road?
- Is there a hotel nearby?
- Excuse me, can you tell me where the closest bank is?
- Are you from around here?
- I am looking for this address.
- Is this the right way to the Railway Station?
- Do you have a map?
- How far is it from here?
- Is it far from here?
- How long does it take to walk there?
- Where is the nearest supermarket?
- Which is the shortest way to the railway station?
- Can you show me on the map?
- Could you tell me how to get to ……?
- Pardon me, I am lost, how do I get to…..?
- What is the best way to…….?

- Where is the Church?
- Can you tell me the way to…..?
- Would you show me the way to the temple?
- Sorry to bother you, but would you mind showing me the way to the railway station?
- Hello! Could you help me? I need to go to the supermarket.
- Hello! Good morning could you tell me how to get to the hospital?

GIVING DIRECTION

- Turn left / right (use when driving only)
- Go right (left, down, up, through)
- Take +road name
- Take the first / second road on the left / right.
- It is on the left.
- Go along the street.
- Go straight ahead…..
- Turn back
- Go back….
- Go straight along the street.
- Go straight and it is on the right.
- Go through the market.
- Go through this passage.
- The easiest way is to….
- The quickest way is to…..
- The best way is to……
- It is in the middle of the block.
- It is on your right / left.
- It is on the corner.

- It is next to / across / between ….. Street name.
- It is on the corner, across from the café.
- It's this way / that way.
- You are going the wrong way.
- You are going the wrong direction.
- Take this road.
- Take the first left…
- Take the first turning on the right / left.
- Take the second on the right….
- Turn right at the cross road.
- Go past the church.
- Go through the market….
- Cross the street.
- Go across the bridge.
- Go as far as the roundabout.
- Turn around.
- Continue past the fire station.
- Continue straight ahead for about a mile.
- It will be on your left / right.
- It'll be straight ahead of you.
- You will see it on your right/left, opposite the hospital / the café.
- You will find it on your right, opposite the church.
- It is just around the corner.
- Not too far.
- About 100 meters.
- It is two blocks away.
- It is in the next street.
- It is just opposite to the church.
- It is at the end of this street.

- It is in the next building.
- It is just behind that church.
- It is very near.
- It is on your left next to the theatre.
- It is on your right next to the park.
- Follow me. I will show you the way.
- Sorry, I am not going in that direction.

USE OF TRANSITION WORDS

- After that take road number 1.
- Then turn right.
- Next you will see.
- When you get to down the hill/slope.
- Finally/after you pass a restaurant on your left take a right at the cross road.
- Then you will see a train station.
- It is behind the hospital.

LANDMARKS

- There is a red building on your right.
- It is across KFC.
- It is diagonally opposite to the post office.
- There is a temple nearby.

WARNINGS

- It is a very busy road.
- It is a one way lane.
- There is traffic in that lane.
- There is an accident.

- There might be road repairs.

If you are new to that place you can say

- I am sorry, I am not from here.
- I am sorry, I am new here.
- I am afraid I cannot help you.
- I don't know my way around.
- Thanks! I have just moved in, so I really don't know my way around yet.

DON'T KNOW

- I have no idea.
- Sorry, I am unsure.
- Please, don't ask me.
- I don't know anything about it.
- I am not sure about that.
- That's a good question. I'll check it out.
- I haven't the idea.
- I don't have any information about that.

19. HELP

- Do you need help?
- Please help me.
- Can you help me, please?
- Can you assist me?
- How can I help you?
- I am happy to help.
- Can I help you with anything?
- Can I ask a favor?

- I need some help, please.
- I can't manage, can you help?
- Could you help me for a second?
- I wonder if you could help me with this.
- Lend me a hand with this, will you?
- I could do with some help, please.
- If you don't mind, I really need your help with……
- Would you mind helping me?
- Do you need help finding anything?
- Give me a hand, please.
- Would you help me?
- Can you do something for me?
- Can you give me a hand with this?
- Could you help me for a second?
- Could you do me a favor?
- Will you help me with this problem?
- I wonder if you could help me with this.
- Glad to help.
- Give me a hand, please.

20. SAY'YES'

- Yes, what can I do for you?
- Yes, what is it?
- Sure I can.
- No problem!
- Definitely!
- I will do it for you.
- I will do it.
- Why not?

- I do.
- Your wish is my command.

21. SAY 'NO'

- No thanks.
- Not this time.
- It's not possible.
- I shall not.
- Not now.
- Certainly not.
- Maybe another time.
- I don't know what to say.
- I wish I could but I have work to do.
- No thanks, I have another commitment.
- Unfortunately, it's not a good time.
- It's not a good idea for me.
- I am not taking on anything else right now.
- I really appreciate you asking me, but I can't do it.
- I can't take on any more responsibilities.
- I'm sorry I'm busy.
- Let me think about that.
- Thanks, but this is not going to work.
- I can help you find a solution.
- I know this is important but I can't.

22. SORRY

- I'm so sorry.
- Excuse me.
- Excuse me, you should not smoke here.

- I deeply regret my actions yesterday.
- Sorry for the trouble.
- I am sorry I am late.
- I am sorry for your inconvenience.
- I am very sorry about the mess.
- I am sorry, I am busy.
- I am very sorry for what I did.
- Sorry, I spill the milk on your shirt.
- I apologized for being late.
- Sorry, I can't talk right now. I am working.

23. ACCEPTING APOLOGY

- Never mind
- It's okay.
- It's fine.
- That's okay.
- Don't worry about it.
- It doesn't matter.
- No problem.
- That's all right.
- I quite understand.
- Forget about it.
- Please don't let it happen again.

24. PHONE CONVERSATION

- Hi, this is Peter.
- Who is this?
- Who is on the phone?
- This is he. Who is calling?

- May I speak with John?
- Is this Mr. Sam?
- Hello, Is John there?
- May I speak to Sam?
- Is John there?
- Hold the line, please.
- Hold on a minute.
- Speaking, who is calling please?
- Who is speaking?
- Yes, this is he.
- Why are you calling me?
- One moment, please.
- Here is my mobile number.
- I tried to call you many times this morning.
- Sorry, I had my phone on mute.
- Sorry, I had an important meeting.
- I need to make a call.
- He is not here. Would you like to leave a message?
- Could you ask him to call me back?
- Thanks for calling.
- This is John speaking.
- Could I speak to Sheela please?
- I am trying to contact Mr. Adam.
- I am calling on behalf of Mr. Smith.
- May I ask who is calling, please?
- Whom would you like to speak?
- I would like to make a reservation please.
- Could you hold on a moment, please?
- Give me a call next time.

- I am afraid my English is not very strong. Could you speak slowly please?
- What is your phone number?
- Can I leave a message, please?
- Thank you for calling.
- Hi, it's John here.
- Is Sam there?
- Who is it?
- Just a minute.
- I will call you later.
- The line is busy now. Please hold the line.
- Okay, wait a moment please.
- John is out at the moment.
- I will call you back soon.
- Sorry, I did not catch that.
- I can't hear you very well.
- Can you give me a call tonight?
- His phone is switched off.
- My battery is dead.
- My battery is low.
- Can I take your name and number?
- Do you have video call in your mobile?
- Let me connect you his department. They will answer your question.
- Your phone is still charging.
- I don't have charger.
- My battery is down.
- I will tell him to call you back when he gets home.
- Signal is weak.

- I don't have signal.
- It is not reachable.
- I lost my phone.
- Give me a call when you reach home.
- Send me a message.
- I'll let you know that you rang.
- Did you catch what I have said?
- My phone doesn't work.
- May I use your mobile, please?
- When is the good time to call you back?
- Talk soon.
- Can I ask who is calling?
- Can I take a message?
- I am sorry, he is out / busy now.
- Could I get your phone number?
- I will let him know you called.
- Will you carry this message for me?
- Okay, let me repeat that just to make sure. (confirming information)
- Would you like to leave a message?
- Could you tell him that I called?
- Give me a missed call.
- Call me in an hour.
- I have the wrong number, sorry.
- What number are you calling?
- Sorry, I got the wrong number.
- Sorry, what did you say?
- I am sorry, I can't hear you.
- Would you mind saying that again?

- Could you spell it, please?
- I cannot hear you very well.
- Will you speak up please?
- Could you repeat your address, please?

25. BUSY

- I am busy.
- He is busy now.
- I am busy right now.
- I don't know whether she is busy or not.
- Are you busy at the moment?
- Are you busy right now?
- I would be happy to help you, but I am very busy.
- Are you busy?
- I am busy today, otherwise I would help.

ARE YOU BUSY

- Do you have a second?
- May I bother you a moment?
- Can you stop for a moment?
- May I have a word with you for a moment?
- Am I disturbing you?
- Are you busy?
- Am I interrupting? (Don't interrupt unless emergency)

26. AIR TRAVEL

- Could I see your boarding pass, please?
- Could I see your passport, please?
- May I have your passport, please?

- How much check-in baggage do you have?
- Are you travelling alone?
- Which class would you like?
- Good morning, Sir. Where are you flying today?
- Do you have any carry-on baggage?
- Is anybody else travelling with you?
- Here is your boarding pass.
- Can I get your ticket number?
- Do you have a visa?
- May I see your passport, please?
- You are scheduled to depart on May 6 at 10 am.
- Would you like the window seat or an aisle seat?
- How much is the fare for a baby?
- It is 20 percent for an adult fare.
- How much is the fare?
- Do you have anything to declare?
- I can give you the aisle seat.
- Your ticket has been confirmed.
- I would like to change my reservation.
- What is your nationality?
- Good morning welcome to A1 airlines.
- Would you like chicken or beef?
- Would you like something to drink?
- Passengers for flight cx831 please proceed to gate number31.
- Please put your bag here.
- How many bags do you have to check in?
- What do you have in your hand bag?
- Where are you flying today?
- Please open your bag.

- Please take off your laptops and mobile phone.
- Put it in this tray.
- You may proceed to the check-in counter.
- You can proceed to the security check.
- I am carrying my backpack into the cabin.
- Your passport is expired.
- Your flight is delayed.
- Your flight cx831 has been delayed.
- Your flight cx831 has been cancelled.
- Flight cj921 is now boarding.
- Please step through the metal detector.
- Passengers may now begin boarding.
- Please give me your ticket and ID.
- Can I see your ID and the ticket please?
- Do you have any check-in baggage?
- Welcome aboard!
- Please put you tray back up.
- Your seat number is 8B.
- Your flight has been cancelled due to the thick fog.
- Please put your seat back in the upright position.
- Please fasten your seatbelts.
- Relax and enjoy the flight.
- We are approaching our destination.
- Would you like a drink or snacks?
- Are you on a vacation or a business trip?
- What is the purpose of your visit business or pleasure?
- How long are you planning to stay?
- Enjoy your flight.

CUSTOMER

- I would like to book a flight to Malaysia.
- I would like to confirm my flight.
- Can we check-in now?
- I need a flight on June 6th.
- Where is the departure gate?
- Is there an airport bus?
- Is my flight on time?
- Can I bring this on plane?
- I will be staying at the hotel.
- Will the flight be delayed?
- Will the flight depart soon?
- When it will take off?
- Will it be ready in ten minutes?
- Will you take me to the airport?
- How long is the flight?
- Here is my ID and my ticket.
- Here is my passport.
- Here it is.
- Where is the boarding gate?
- My passport is expiring can I still travel.
- Could you show me where to sit?
- Would you please get me a blanket?
- Could we change our seats, please?
- Could I have a window seat, please?
- Where is the taxi stand?
- Where is immigration?
- Where can I get the visa?
- Where can we exchange our money?

- We lost our bags.
- I lost my bag.
- We are traveling together.
- I have two bags to check-in.
- I don't feel well.
- We missed our flight.
- May I have another drink?
- I'll have the chicken, please.
- I would like a cup of tea, please.
- Do you mind if I put my seat back?
- Can you translate it into English?
- I have just arrived at the airport.
- I feel ill.
- Can I have a pillow?
- My headphone doesn't work.
- At what time do we land?
- What time does the flight leave?
- We have nothing to declare.
- Where is the arrival gate?
- We are here on holiday/on business.
- We need a taxi.

27. BUS– TRAIN– TAXI

- Where is the ticket counter?
- Where is the bus stop?
- Where can I buy tickets from?
- Can I buy tickets on the bus?
- What time is the next bus to Kerala?
- How much is a single ticket to Chennai?

- How much is a return ticket to Mumbai?
- I would like a single ticket to Karnataka?
- How much is a child single ticket to Bangalore?
- How much is a first class single ticket to Chennai?
- How often do the trains/buses run to Chennai?
- Where is the bus stop?
- Which bus should I take?
- Do you know where the bus stop is?
- The bus will be here soon.
- Here comes the bus.
- I take this bus every day.
- How long have you been waiting.
- You can buy your ticket at the station.
- How much is the ticket?
- How can I get there?
- Is this the way to ……?
- Is it possible to change the ticket?
- How often does this bus run?
- I missed my train.
- I missed my stop.
- I missed my usual bus.
- It takes 30 minutes to go to the station.
- Is there a bus stop near here?
- Does this bus go to University?
- Is anybody else travelling with you?
- Does the bus stop at the railway station?
- How much is a bus ticket?
- Can you show me the way to the nearest bus station?
- I took a bus to work this morning.

- The bus fare is high.
- Could you tell me which platform I should go to?
- The train has not arrived yet.
- It is always crowded in the bus.
- I have to stand all the way.
- Does this bus run past the High court?
- I am on a train.
- The ticket counter is very crowd.
- I can’t get the ticket.
- I booked the ticket in online.
- I would like to rent a car.
- Do you have a driving license?
- I can return it in one week.
- Where can I find a taxi stand?
- Please tell me where a taxi stand is.
- Would you call a taxi for me, please?
- Please hail a taxi.
- How long does it take by taxi/bus?
- Do you mind parking my car here?
- Could you get a taxi for me?
- Take me to this address, please.
- Take me there, please.
- I need to go to this address.
- You should go there by taxi.
- Shall I take a taxi?
- I left my purse in the taxi.
- Do you know where the taxi stand is?
- Is that taxi occupied?
- Is it far from here?

- How long does it take to get there?
- How far is it from hotel to the airport?
- How far is it from here?
- How far is it from here to the station?
- I need to go to this address.
- Could you drive a bit faster?
- I am in a hurry.
- How many hours it will take?
- How many kilometers are there?
- It will take half an hour, Sir.
- Ok, let's go.
- Could you stop here, please?
- Please stop here.
- Right here, please.
- How much should I pay?
- How much?

28. TRAFFIC

- There is a traffic jam on the highway.
- I got stuck in traffic.
- I was caught in traffic.
- The traffic was terrible.
- It is like a car park.
- I was delayed by a traffic jam.
- The traffic was slow.

29. BUSINESS CONVERSATION

Conversation 1: Meeting

Manager : Good morning, everyone. Let's start the meeting.
Employee 1 : Good morning, sir. What is today's agenda?
Manager : We need to discuss the new project.
Employee 2 : What is the deadline for this project?
Manager : The deadline is the 30th of this month.
Employee 1 : Should we prepare a report for the client?
Manager : Yes, please prepare it by next week.
Employee 2 : Who will present the report in the meeting?
Manager : You will present it, and your team will support you.
Employee 1 : Okay sir, we will start working on it today.

Conversation 2: Phone Call in Office

Receptionist : Good afternoon, ABC Company. How may I help you?
Client : Hello, I want to speak with the manager.
Receptionist : May I know who is calling, please?
Client : This is Mr. Kumar from Global Traders.
Receptionist : Thank you. Please hold the line for a moment.
Manager : Hello, this is the manager speaking.
Client : Good afternoon. I would like to confirm our meeting tomorrow.
Manager : Yes, the meeting is at 11 a.m. in our office.
Client : Perfect, I will be there on time.
Manager : Thank you, see you tomorrow.

Conversation 3: Asking About Workload

Employee : Good morning, sir. Do you have any tasks for me today?
Manager : Yes, please check the new emails first.
Employee : Should I reply to all of them?
Manager : No, just reply to the important ones.
Employee : Okay, and what about the pending reports?
Manager : Finish them before lunch if possible.
Employee : Alright, I will try my best.
Manager : After lunch, prepare a summary for the meeting.
Employee : Sure, I will complete it on time.
Manager : Good, thank you for your hard work.

Conversation 4: Deadline Discussion

Manager : How is the project going?
Employee : We have completed 70% of the work.
Manager : That's good, but the deadline is very close.
Employee : Yes sir, we are working extra hours.
Manager : Do you need more support from the team?
Employee : If possible, one more person can help us.
Manager : Okay, I will assign Mr. Ravi to your team.
Employee : Thank you, that will speed up the work.
Manager : Please make sure to finish before Friday.
Employee : Don't worry sir, we will complete it on time.

Conversation 5: Teamwork Discussion

Manager : Good morning, team. Are you ready for today's work?
Employee 1 : Yes sir, we have divided the tasks.

Employee 2 : I will handle the data entry part.
Employee 3 : And I will prepare the presentation slides.
Manager : Very good. Who will contact the client?
Employee 1 : I will call the client and confirm the details.
Manager : Excellent. Please keep me updated on the progress.
Employee 2 : Sure sir, we will send you reports every evening.
Manager : That's great teamwork. Keep it up.
Employees : Thank you, sir. We will do our best.

Conversation 6: Asking for Leave

Employee : Good morning, sir. May I talk to you for a minute?
Manager : Yes, please go ahead.
Employee : I need leave on Monday due to a family function.
Manager : Okay, how many days of leave do you need?
Employee : Just one day, sir.
Manager : Alright, but submit a leave request to HR.
Employee : Sure sir, I will do it today.
Manager : Also, finish your pending tasks before you go.
Employee : Don't worry sir, I will complete them.
Manager : Good, enjoy your day with your family.

Conversation 7: Client Visit

Manager : Good afternoon, welcome to our office.
Client : Good afternoon, thank you for inviting me.
Manager : Please have a seat. Would you like some coffee or tea?
Client : A cup of coffee would be nice, thank you.
Manager : Sure, I will ask the staff to bring it.
Client : I have reviewed your proposal. It looks interesting.
Manager : I'm glad to hear that. Do you have any suggestions?

Client	:	Yes, we can reduce the timeline by two weeks.
Manager	:	That sounds good. We will adjust our plan.
Client	:	Perfect. I look forward to working with you.

Conversation 8: Performance Review

Manager	:	Please sit down, we need to discuss your performance.
Employee	:	Yes sir, I'm ready.
Manager	:	Your work has been good this quarter.
Employee	:	Thank you, I tried my best.
Manager	:	You completed projects on time and supported your team.
Employee	:	I always focus on teamwork, sir.
Manager	:	That's excellent. However, you can improve your communication.
Employee	:	I understand, I will work on it.
Manager	:	Good. We are considering you for a promotion.
Employee	:	Thank you very much, sir. I really appreciate it.

Conversation 9: Office Training

Trainer	:	Welcome everyone to the training session.
Employee 1	:	Thank you, we are excited to learn.
Trainer	:	Today, we will cover safety rules in the office.
Employee 2	:	Will you also explain the emergency exits?
Trainer	:	Yes, I will show you the exit points.
Employee 1	:	How long will this session take?
Trainer	:	Around one hour, including questions.
Employee 2	:	Can we get training materials later?
Trainer	:	Of course, I will share them by email.
Employees	:	Great, thank you for your support.

Conversation 10: Office Canteen

Employee 1 : Hi, are you going for lunch now?
Employee 2 : Yes, I was just about to leave.
Employee 1 : Let's go together to the canteen.
Employee 2 : Sure, what will you eat today?
Employee 1 : I think I'll try the special meal.
Employee 2 : Good idea, I heard it's tasty.
Employee 1 : Do you usually eat here or bring food from home?
Employee 2 : Mostly I eat here, it saves time.
Employee 1 : That's true. The prices are reasonable too.
Employee 2 : Yes, and the coffee here is also very good.

30. BASIC BUSINESS VOCABULARY

Client – A person who buys services.

Customer – A person who buys goods.

Colleague – A person you work with.

Employer – A person or company that hires people.

Employee – A person who works for a company.

Boss – The person in charge.

Manager – A person who controls a team or department.

Team – A group of people working together.

Office – A place where people work.

Workplace – The location of your job.

Meeting – A gathering to discuss work.

Discussion – Talking about a topic.

Agenda – A list of items to discuss in a meeting.

Minutes – Notes of what was discussed in a meeting.

Deadline – The last date to finish work.

Target – A goal to achieve.

Goal – Something you aim to reach.

Project – A planned piece of work.

Task – A piece of work to do.

Workload – The amount of work to do.

Overtime – Extra hours of work.

Shift – A set working time.

Training – Teaching skills for a job.

Intern – A student working for experience.

Probation – A trial period at a new job.

Salary – Monthly pay for a job.

Wages – Money earned by the hour or day.

Bonus – Extra money for good work.

Leave – Permission to be absent from work.

Holiday – A day when you don't work.

Promotion – Moving to a higher position.

Demotion – Moving to a lower position.

Transfer – Moving to another job/place.

Resignation – Leaving a job by choice.

Retirement – Stopping work permanently.

Termination – Ending someone's job.

Vacancy – An empty job position.

Recruitment – Process of hiring people.

Hiring – Giving someone a job.

Interview – A meeting to select candidates.

Application – A request for a job.

Experience – Knowledge gained from work.

Qualification – Education or skills needed.

Reference – A recommendation from someone.

Certificate – An official document of skills.

Conference – A formal meeting.

Seminar – A small training event.

Workshop – A hands-on training session.

Presentation – Showing information to others.

Report – A written document with details.

Memo – A short office message.

Notice – An official announcement.

Circular – A message sent to many people.

Policy – A company's rules or guidelines.

Procedure – A step-by-step process.

Rules – Instructions to follow.

Regulations – Official rules.

Contract – A written legal agreement.

Agreement – A mutual decision between parties.

Deal – A business arrangement.

Partnership – A business shared by two or more people.

Shareholder – A person who owns company shares.

Investor – A person who puts money into a business.

Stakeholder – A person affected by a company's actions.

Supplier – A person/company providing goods.

Vendor – A seller of products.

Distributor – A person/company that delivers goods.

Franchise – A licensed business model.

Merger – Joining of two companies.

Acquisition – One company taking over another.

Entrepreneur – A person who starts a business.

Start-up – A newly formed business.

Innovation – A new idea or method.

Strategy – A long-term plan.

Planning – Organizing work in advance.

Execution – Carrying out a plan.

Leadership – Guiding and motivating people.

Delegation – Giving tasks to others.

Motivation – Encouragement to work harder.

Productivity – How much work is done in a time.

Efficiency – Doing work in the best way.

Quality – The standard of something.

Standards – Accepted levels of quality.

Benchmark – A point of comparison.

Performance – How well someone works.

Appraisal – A review of performance.

Feedback – Comments about performance.

Audit – An official financial check.

Budget – A financial spending plan.

Expenditure – Money spent.

Revenue – Money earned by a company.

Income – Money received.

Profit – Money gained after expenses.

Loss – Money wasted or not gained.

Assets – Things owned with value.

Yours sincerely,
[Your Name]

8. Recommendation Letter

Subject: Recommendation for Mr. Ravi

Dear Sir/Madam,
I am pleased to recommend Mr. Ravi for the position of Marketing Manager. He has shown great dedication and skill in his work during his tenure with us.

Yours sincerely,
[Your Name]

9. Invitation Letter

Subject: Invitation to Annual Business Meet

Dear Sir,
We are pleased to invite you to our Annual Business Meet to be held on [date] at [venue]. We look forward to your presence.

Yours sincerely,
[Your Name]

10. Acknowledgement Letter

Subject: Acknowledgement of Payment Received

Dear Sir,
We acknowledge the receipt of your payment of ₹80,000 towards invoice no. 6567. Thank you for your prompt payment.

Yours sincerely,
[Your Name]

11. Letter to Open a Savings Account

From
Rohan
12, Guru Apartment 2nd floor,
Lake View Street,
Bangalore.
To
The Branch Manager
45, Town Hall Road
Nethaji Street
Bangalore

Subject: Request to open a savings account

Respected Sir,
I would like to open a savings account in your branch. Please find enclosed the required documents, photographs, and completed application form.

Kindly process my request at the earliest.

Thanking you,
Yours faithfully,
Rohan

12. Letter to Close Bank Account

Subject: Request to close my bank account
Respected Sir/Madam,

I have been maintaining a savings account with your branch (A/c No: ____________). I would like to close this account due to personal reasons. Please transfer the remaining balance to me in cash/cheque.

Thanking you,

13. Letter for Loan Request

Subject: Request for loan

Respected Madam,
I am maintaining a savings account with your branch for the past five years. I request you to kindly grant me a personal loan of Rs. 200000.
I assure you of timely repayment.

Enclosed are the required documents for your reference.

Thanking you,

14. Letter to Open a Current Account

Subject: Request to open a current account

Respected Sir,
I wish to open a current account in the name of my business [Business Name].
I am enclosing the application form along with the necessary documents.
Kindly do the needful.

15. Letter to Block a Lost ATM Card

Subject: Request to block lost ATM card

Respected Sir,

I hold a savings account with your branch (A/c No: ____________).
Unfortunately, I lost my ATM card yesterday. I request you to kindly block the card immediately to prevent misuse.

Please issue me a new ATM card at the earliest.

Thanking you,

16. Letter for Education Loan

Subject: Request for education loan

Respected Sir,
I am a student admitted to [College Name] for the course [Course Name]. I request you to kindly grant me an education loan of Rs. 300000 to support my studies.
I have attached admission proof, fee structure, and other required documents.

Thanking you,

17. Letter for Fixed Deposit Creation

Subject: Request to open fixed deposit

Respected Sir,
I am an account holder in your branch (A/c No: 88852222). I request you to kindly open a fixed deposit account in my name for an amount of Rs. 8500000 for a period of 10 years.

Thanking you,

IT SECTOR

General Office Communication

- I just logged into my system.
- Let's start the day's work.
- Did you check your emails?
- I will update you once it's done.
- Please share the latest report.
- Can you send me the link?
- I will join the meeting in five minutes.
- Let's discuss this after lunch.
- I'm working on that task right now.
- Please check the shared folder.
- I will ping you once it's ready.
- Can you review this document?
- I will upload it to the drive.
- Please confirm once you receive it.
- Let's have a quick sync-up.
- I am waiting for your feedback.
- I will send you the updated version.
- The file is too large to attach.
- Can you please approve this?
- I am still waiting for access.
- The server is down right now.
- I am debugging the issue.
- The code is running fine now.
- I need to check the error log.
- Please restart the application.
- The system is taking too long to load.

- I am pushing the code to GitHub.
- Please pull the latest changes.
- The database connection failed.
- I am updating the configuration file.
- The build is successful.
- The deployment failed due to an error.
- I will rollback the changes.
- We need to merge the branches.
- Please clear your cache and try again.
- The API is not responding.
- I'll raise a ticket for that.
- The network seems slow today.
- Let's check the server status.
- The software needs an update.
- Let's divide the work among us.
- Can we have a quick call to discuss?
- Please keep me in the loop.
- I will coordinate with the testing team.
- Let's review the progress tomorrow.
- Please assign this task to me.
- I will handle this part.
- Can you take care of the documentation?
- Let's finalize the design first.
- Please share your screen.
- I will present the demo.
- Let's fix the bugs before release.
- Please follow up with the client.
- I will update the tracker.
- Let's create a new branch for this feature.

- Please commit your changes.
- We need to follow the process.
- Let's add this to our sprint.
- I'll inform the manager.
- Please close the ticket once verified.
- Can you hear me clearly?
- Let's start with a quick update.
- Yesterday I worked on the login module.
- Today I will focus on the dashboard.
- I am facing an issue with the API.
- I will check with the backend team.
- The testing is in progress.
- We will deploy it tomorrow.
- Let's discuss the project timeline.
- The client meeting is scheduled at 3 p.m.
- Please prepare the presentation slides.
- Let's review the requirements once again.
- The demo went well.
- We received positive feedback.
- Let's work on the changes.
- Please summarize the meeting notes.
- I'll share the MOM (Minutes of Meeting).
- Let's plan for the next release.
- The deadline is approaching.
- Please find the attached file.
- Kindly review and revert.
- Thank you for your quick response.
- Please let me know your availability.
- I appreciate your support.

- I will get back to you soon.
- Please acknowledge receipt.
- Sorry for the delay in response.
- Please check and confirm.
- Awaiting your approval.
- Thanks for the update.
- Please share your feedback.
- I will revert with details.
- Kindly note the changes.
- Thank you for your patience.
- Please reply at your earliest convenience.
- I will keep you informed.
- Please mark a copy to the manager.
- Let's close this discussion.
- Have a great day ahead.
- I am writing the backend logic.
- The frontend looks good now.
- I need to fix some UI issues.
- The function is not returning the expected value.
- Let's refactor the code.
- Please add proper comments.
- The version control is not updated.
- The build pipeline needs configuration.
- I will check the API response.
- The script is throwing an error.
- Let's optimize the performance.
- The test cases passed successfully.
- We need to handle exceptions.
- Please use proper naming conventions.

- I will create a pull request.
- The feature is ready for review.
- Let’s fix the minor bugs.
- The deployment is scheduled for tonight.
- I will test it in staging.
- The production environment looks stable.
- Please restart your computer.
- Did you check the network connection?
- Try clearing your cookies.
- The printer is not working.
- I will raise a service request.
- The system needs antivirus update.
- Your account has been locked.
- Please reset your password.
- The email server is not reachable.
- I will check the system logs.
- Please reinstall the software.
- The laptop needs repair.
- The issue is resolved now.
- Please test it and confirm.
- The update will take a few minutes.
- Please connect to the VPN.
- The remote desktop is not responding.
- I will escalate this issue.
- The IT support team is working on it.
- Please report any other issues.
- We are behind schedule.
- Let’s plan the next sprint.
- The project is in phase two.

- Please update the task status.
- The milestone has been achieved.
- We need client approval.
- Let's review the project scope.
- Please update the progress tracker.
- The timeline is tight.
- Let's prioritize the tasks.
- The budget has been approved.
- We will start the next phase soon.
- Please share the project report.
- Let's assign responsibilities.
- The risk needs to be mitigated.
- We will monitor the progress weekly.
- Please prepare the documentation.
- The final review is tomorrow.
- The client requested a change.
- Let's update the project plan.
- Thank you for your valuable feedback.
- We will make the necessary changes.
- The new feature is under development.
- We will deliver it by Friday.
- Please confirm your requirements.
- The testing is almost complete.
- The report will be shared soon.
- We will schedule a demo tomorrow.
- Please share your observations.
- We will fix the issues immediately.
- The delay was due to dependency.
- We appreciate your understanding.

- The updated file has been shared.
- Please let us know if you face any issues.
- The support team will assist you.
- The performance has been improved.
- The project is on track.
- Thank you for your continued support.
- We value your partnership.
- Looking forward to your feedback.
- I am attending a training session.
- The topic is about cloud computing.
- I learned something new today.
- Please share the training materials.
- The session was very informative.
- I will practice the examples later.
- The trainer explained it clearly.
- The certification is useful for my career.
- Let's apply this concept in our project.
- I'll prepare notes for the team.
- We have a workshop next week.
- The course is almost complete.
- I am improving my coding skills.
- Please help me understand this topic.
- I will take an online course.
- The trainer will share the recordings.
- It's a hands-on training.
- Let's complete the assignments.
- The exam is scheduled tomorrow.
- I passed the certification exam.
- I completed the assigned task.

- The update has been pushed.
- I am working on the next module.
- The review is pending.
- Please approve the changes.
- The testing team is verifying it.
- I fixed the reported bug.
- The issue is no longer reproducible.
- I have added the missing files.
- The code quality has improved.
- Please update the changelog.
- I will document the process.
- The review comments are implemented.
- Please validate the fix.
- The new version is ready.
- Let's release it tomorrow.
- I'll inform the QA team.
- The results look perfect.
- Everything is working fine now.
- Great job, team!
- I will finish it before the deadline.
- The task will take two hours.
- I'm running out of time.
- Let's schedule it for tomorrow.
- Please remind me later.
- I will set a reminder.
- Let's plan our tasks properly.
- I need an extension for this task.
- The work is almost done.
- I will complete it after the meeting.

- The deadline has been extended.
- Let's focus on high priority tasks.
- The project needs more resources.
- I'll take a short break.
- Let's work on it after lunch.
- I am multitasking right now.
- Please prioritize this issue.
- I will update you by end of the day.
- The task took longer than expected.
- Finally, it's completed.
- Please share the analytics report.
- The data looks accurate.
- We need to clean the dataset.
- The report will be auto-generated.
- The dashboard is updated daily.
- Let's visualize the results.
- The graph shows good progress.
- Please verify the data entries.
- The statistics are impressive.
- Let's export it to Excel.
- The query took too long to execute.
- I will check the database schema.
- The report is ready for review.
- Let's share it with the management.
- Please include last month's data.
- The KPI values are on target.
- We need to fix the formula.
- The data backup is complete.
- Please check the logs for errors.

- Everything looks fine in the report.
- I will be late today.
- I am working from home.
- Please mark me present.
- The attendance system is not working.
- I will apply for leave tomorrow.
- Please approve my leave request.
- I will come early tomorrow.
- The meeting room is booked.
- Let's move to the conference room.
- I will get a coffee and join.
- The office Wi-Fi is slow.
- Please connect to the projector.
- The AC is too cold here.
- Let's order lunch together.
- I am logging off for the day.
- Please lock your system before leaving.
- I will work overtime today.
- The weekend starts tomorrow.
- See you on Monday!
- That's a great idea.
- I completely agree with you.
- Let's do it that way.
- I will make the necessary changes.
- Please double-check it.
- That's not part of our scope.
- Let's confirm with the manager.
- We should test it thoroughly.
- That's a temporary fix.

- The final version looks perfect.
- Please keep it confidential.
- That's beyond our control.
- We need more information.
- Let's clarify the requirement.
- Please share your thoughts.
- Let's take a short break.
- We will continue after this.
- I really appreciate your help.
- It has been a productive day.
- Please update your timesheet.
- I'm checking the project tracker.
- Let's align our schedules.
- Can you please mute your mic?
- You're on mute, I can't hear you.
- Please turn on your camera.
- I will share my screen now.
- The connection is unstable.
- Let's reconnect after a few minutes.
- Can you resend the invitation link?
- The meeting ID is not working.
- Let's reschedule the meeting.
- Please send the meeting summary.
- I missed the call, sorry about that.
- Let's discuss this one-on-one.
- Please note down the action points.
- I will add it to our to-do list.
- Let's finalize it today.
- I will take care of this task.

- I will handle it from my end.
- Please keep me posted.
- Let's set up a recurring meeting.
- I will forward this email to you.
- Let's close this topic for now.
- Please share your availability.
- The meeting was very productive.
- Let's have a follow-up call.
- Please document the discussion.
- I will update the minutes of meeting.
- Let's have a brainstorming session.
- We need a proper plan of action.
- I will notify the team immediately.
- Please avoid last-minute changes.
- Let's keep this as a low priority.
- I will escalate it to the manager.
- Please loop in the concerned team.
- Let's track the progress daily.
- I will create a separate task for it.
- We will discuss this offline.
- Thanks everyone for joining!
- I am updating the code repository.
- The merge conflict needs resolution.
- Please review my pull request.
- The API key has expired.
- I will check the authentication token.
- The function is returning null.
- Let's debug it step by step.
- I will add a console log to verify.

- The syntax error is fixed.
- The build pipeline failed.
- I will restart the CI/CD process.
- The compiler shows a warning.
- I will check for memory leaks.
- The script needs optimization.
- The variable is undefined.
- Please re-run the test cases.
- I will check the dependency version.
- The module import failed.
- Let’s review the algorithm.
- The function parameters are incorrect.
- I will use a different logic.
- Please create a backup before changes.
- The patch has been applied.
- The update is pushed to production.
- The rollback was successful.
- Let’s test it in the staging environment.
- The API call is taking too long.
- I will add retry logic to it.
- The application crashed unexpectedly.
- The bug has been reproduced.
- I will fix it in the next commit.
- Please clear the temporary files.
- I will check the configuration path.
- The UI alignment looks off.
- Please test it on multiple browsers.
- The layout is not responsive.
- Let’s check it on mobile view.

- I will optimize the database query.
- The code is now more efficient.
- Everything is working perfectly now.
- Please join the daily stand-up.
- Let's go around for quick updates.
- I completed my yesterday's tasks.
- Today I will work on bug fixes.
- I am waiting for the QA feedback.
- No blockers from my side.
- I will support the testing team.
- Let's plan the next sprint goals.
- Please assign the new story to me.
- The backlog needs to be refined.
- I will add it to the Jira board.
- Please change the task status to "In Progress."
- The sprint review went well.
- Let's prepare for sprint planning.
- We completed all stories on time.
- Please mention it in the retrospective.
- The team performed really well.
- Let's improve our workflow.
- Please document your learning's.
- I will help you with that issue.
- Let's pair program for this task.
- Please update your progress daily.
- I will follow up on your pending tasks.
- Let's keep our communication open.
- Please maintain the code standards.
- I will share my suggestions later.

- Let's test it together.
- I appreciate your hard work.
- The teamwork was excellent.
- Let's celebrate our success.
- We'll learn from our mistakes.
- Let's aim for better quality next time.
- Please give your honest feedback.
- I will take note of that.
- That's a great point, thank you.
- Let's agree on the next steps.
- Please share your ideas freely.
- I completely support your view.
- Let's finalize it by tomorrow.
- Thank you, team, for your effort!
- Thank you for reaching out to us.
- We are looking into the issue.
- The problem will be resolved soon.
- We appreciate your patience.
- Please share a screenshot of the error.
- Could you please explain the issue in detail?
- We will get back to you shortly.
- The update has been successfully deployed.
- The issue is fixed in the latest version.
- Please clear your browser cache.
- Kindly refresh and check again.
- Thank you for confirming.
- We will monitor it for a few more days.
- The new feature is now available.
- Please try it and share your feedback.

- The bug was caused by a configuration error.
- We have taken corrective measures.
- The downtime was minimal.
- We have improved system performance.
- Please let us know if the problem persists.
- The request has been acknowledged.
- We will provide an update soon.
- The migration process is complete.
- Please test it in your environment.
- We value your continued trust.
- Thank you for your understanding.
- The data has been restored successfully.
- Please verify the output.
- Your satisfaction is our priority.
- We appreciate your feedback and cooperation.
- We will send you the final invoice.
- Please share the payment confirmation.
- The project is officially closed.
- Thank you for working with us.
- We hope to collaborate again.
- Please contact our support for further help.
- We will ensure this doesn’t happen again.
- The client meeting went smoothly.
- They were happy with our progress.
- The client approved the final version.
- Let’s identify the root cause.
- Please reproduce the issue.
- I will check the logs for errors.
- Let’ verify it step by step.

- I think it's a configuration issue.
- The error message is not clear.
- I will do a deep analysis.
- Please restart the application once.
- Let's check if the file is corrupted.
- I will clear the cache and try again.
- It seems to be a network problem.
- Please disconnect and reconnect.
- I will check the service status.
- The firewall might be blocking it.
- The system is running out of memory.
- Let's check the disk space.
- The backup didn't complete properly.
- Please reinstall the driver.
- The patch fixed the issue.
- I will test it after reboot.
- The issue occurs only sometimes.
- Let's compare both environments.
- I will update the dependencies.
- Please provide the log file.
- The error code indicates a timeout.
- Let's check the configuration path.
- I will test it in a different system.
- The issue was caused by a missing file.
- The network latency is too high.
- I will contact the infrastructure team.
- The fix is deployed successfully.
- The system is working fine now.
- Please confirm the resolution.

- Let's document the root cause.
- I will close the incident ticket.
- The issue has been permanently resolved.
- Everything is stable now.
- Thank you for verifying it.
- Let's prevent this in the future.
- Good job resolving that so quickly!
- Let's start the project review meeting.
- Can you share the project status update?
- The development phase is almost complete.
- We are facing some issues in the testing stage.
- The client requested a few changes in the UI.
- Please update the latest progress on Jira.
- Let's discuss the pending tasks for this sprint.
- We need to finalize the deployment plan.
- The timeline is getting tight; let's prioritize the tasks.
- I'll prepare the project summary by end of the day.
- Please share the latest code changes in GitHub.
- The QA team will start testing tomorrow.
- We have achieved 80% of the sprint goals.
- Let's schedule a demo with the client.
- We need to improve communication between teams.
- Can you prepare the sprint retrospective points?
- The project is on track as per the plan.
- We should discuss the risks and dependencies.
- The UI/UX team has shared new wireframes.
- Let's document all the changes properly.
- The deployment pipeline failed last night.
- Can you check the Jenkins build logs?

- We need to automate this process using Ansible.
- The Docker container is not responding properly.
- Let's restart the Kubernetes pods.
- We should use version control for all configuration files.
- The production server needs an urgent patch update.
- Please verify the CI/CD pipeline setup.
- The build was successful but tests failed.
- Let's roll back to the previous stable version.
- The deployment is scheduled for tonight.
- Can we set up monitoring with Prometheus and Grafana?
- Please check the server load and memory usage.
- We'll move to the cloud environment next week.
- The logs show multiple failed API calls.
- We need to improve release automation.
- Jenkins is throwing a permission denied error.
- Please update the environment variables.
- The deployment was completed without any downtime.
- Let's optimize the Docker image size.
- We are using AWS for our cloud hosting.
- Please create a new EC2 instance for testing.
- The S3 bucket access policy needs to be updated.
- We will use AWS Lambda for automation tasks.
- The Azure subscription is expiring soon.
- Can you enable auto-scaling for the web servers?
- We should back up the database regularly to the cloud.
- The load balancer is not distributing traffic evenly.
- Let's check the cloud cost reports for this month.
- The API gateway is blocking some requests.
- Please configure the IAM roles carefully.

- The network latency is high between regions.
- We need to migrate our database to AWS RDS.
- Let's create a Cloud Formation template for infrastructure.
- The GCP storage usage exceeded our budget.
- Can you enable logging in CloudWatch?
- The virtual machine needs to be resized.
- Let's move to a hybrid cloud setup.
- We should use Terraform for provisioning.
- The SSL certificate is about to expire.
- Let's review the project roadmap for the next quarter.
- We need to allocate more resources to this module.
- The client feedback has been positive so far.
- Please share the updated budget report.
- We should plan the next release timeline.
- The deadlines are approaching; let's stay focused.
- Can we arrange a quick sync-up meeting?
- The manager appreciated our last release.
- Please send the weekly report by Friday.
- Let's discuss the performance metrics.
- We need better time management in this sprint.
- The stakeholder meeting is scheduled for Monday.
- Can you prepare a presentation for tomorrow?
- The escalation issue has been resolved.
- Let's appreciate the team's hard work.
- We need to track the key deliverables.
- The documentation needs to be updated.
- Please assign the new tasks in the tracker.
- The project is moving as per the timeline.
- We must improve the overall code quality.

- Please check your email for the meeting invite.
- The system is running a bit slow today.
- Can you share your screen for a minute?
- Let's connect on Teams after lunch.
- I will raise a ticket for the IT support team.
- The VPN connection is not stable.
- Please restart your system and try again.
- The software update requires a reboot.
- We need admin access for installation.
- Can you clear the cache and try again?
- The printer is not connected to the network.
- Please check the firewall settings.
- The internet speed is quite low today.
- Let's move this discussion to a call.
- I will check the logs and get back to you.
- Please update your antivirus software.
- The patch update will be rolled out tonight.
- The system maintenance is scheduled for Sunday.
- Please close all background applications.
- Everything looks good now — issue resolved.
- What's the color theme for this project?
- Could you send me the logo file?
- I will start working on the layout today.
- The client asked for a few changes.
- Can you review this draft?
- I will make the revisions now.
- The design looks clean and minimal.
- Let's keep the font consistent.
- Please align the text properly.

- The background looks too dark.
- Can we make the image brighter?
- The spacing needs improvement.
- Let's reduce the font size.
- Please increase the padding.
- The color doesn't match the brand guide.
- I will fix the alignment issue.
- This version looks better than before.
- Please send me the high-resolution image.
- What format do you want the file in — JPG or PNG?
- I will export the final design in PDF.
- The layout looks unbalanced.
- Try using a lighter shade.
- Can we add some white space?
- The image is getting cropped.
- I will adjust the margins.
- Please check the typography.
- The header looks great.
- The footer needs some improvement.
- Let's change the button color.
- Can you make the logo smaller?
- This design is mobile-friendly.
- The user interface is very smooth.
- Let's test the design on different screens.
- I will upload the files to the drive.
- The mockup is ready.
- Can you approve this version?
- The feedback was positive.
- I will implement the client's suggestions.

- Let’s finalize the banner today.
- Please update the image in the hero section.
- The proportions are not accurate.
- Let’s add some animation effects.
- The design must look professional.
- Can we use a different font style?
- The icons look outdated.
- I will replace them with modern ones.
- Let’s check the alignment in preview mode.
- I will send the editable file.
- The color combination looks attractive.
- Please avoid too many gradients.
- This page looks cluttered.
- Let’s simplify the layout.
- The banner text is not readable.
- I will fix the contrast issue.
- The design should match the company theme.
- Can you add a border around the image?
- Please move the logo to the top left corner.
- Let’s use a transparent background.
- The client prefers a minimal design.
- I will redesign it from scratch.
- Please remove the watermark.
- The image resolution is too low.
- Let’s check the file size.
- I will compress the image.
- Can we use a different layout?
- The prototype is almost done.
- I will send the Figma link.

- Please add hover effects to the buttons.
- The design looks responsive now.
- Let's change the font to Sans Serif.
- I will align the icons properly.
- The color palette looks perfect.
- Please center the heading.
- The background image looks pixelated.
- Let's reduce the opacity.
- Can we add a call-to-action button?
- The client needs it by tomorrow.
- I will finish the revisions tonight.
- Please share your feedback soon.
- Let's use brand colors only.
- The shadows look too heavy.
- Please lighten them a bit.
- The gradient transition isn't smooth.
- I will fix it right away.
- The banner dimensions are 1080 × 1080.
- Please check the bleed area.
- The print version is ready.
- Let's review the final copy.
- I will upload it to Canva.
- Please send me the PSD file.
- The layers are well organized.
- The text overlaps with the image.
- I will adjust the line spacing.
- Please keep the design simple and clean.
- Let's use the same template for all posts.
- The preview looks amazing.

- I will send the final version for approval.
- Great job! The design looks professional.
- Let's deliver it to the client now.
- We need to increase our social media presence.
- Let's post this on all our social platforms.
- Can you schedule the post for tomorrow?
- Please write a catchy caption for this image.
- Don't forget to add relevant hash tags.
- Let's boost this post to reach more people.
- The engagement rate is going up.
- Our followers are growing slowly.
- This video is getting many views.
- The post didn't perform well.
- Let's review the social media strategy.
- What's our target audience for this campaign?
- Please share the analytics report.
- We should focus more on Instagram this month.
- Let's plan the content calendar for next week.
- Can you check the comments and reply politely?
- The client wants more organic reach.
- We need to improve our content quality.
- Please update me on the ad performance.
- Let's have a quick brainstorming session.
- Let's run a paid campaign on Facebook.
- What's the budget for this ad?
- The click-through rate is improving.
- We are getting more conversions from Instagram.
- Please optimize the ad copy.
- Try changing the thumbnail image.

- We need a strong call-to-action.
- Can we target a younger audience?
- The ROI looks promising.
- This post needs better visuals.
- Let's make a short reel for engagement.
- Try using trending audio for this reel.
- The caption should be more emotional.
- Let's create a carousel post.
- Can you design a story template?
- Add our logo to the image.
- Keep the tone friendly and positive.
- This meme could go viral.
- Let's create a brand awareness video.
- We should analyze the insights weekly.
- What's our engagement rate this month?
- The post reached 20,000 people organically.
- Let's compare this campaign with the previous one.
- We need to study the competitors' strategies.
- The audience prefers short videos.
- Let's track our hashtag performance.
- Our content needs more consistency.
- Engagement dropped after changing the timing.
- Let's post when our audience is most active.
- We should interact more with followers.
- Reply to all messages within an hour.
- Keep the comments section positive.
- Handle negative comments professionally.
- Let's collaborate with influencers.
- That influencer has a good reach.

- We can do a giveaway campaign.
- The feedback is mostly positive.
- Let's thank followers for their support.
- Brand reputation is very important.
- The monthly report is ready.
- We gained 400 new followers this week.
- The engagement rate improved by 15%.
- The ad campaign reached 10,000 people.
- The client is happy with the results.
- Let's prepare a presentation for the client.
- Please include screenshots of analytics.
- We need to show the growth clearly.
- Let's summarize the performance in one slide.
- The report should look professional.
- Let's finalize the content ideas today.
- Please share your designs before posting.
- We will post three times a week.
- Let's plan a festival campaign.
- Please check the spelling before posting.
- Schedule the post at 10 a.m.
- Tag our partners in the post.
- Don't forget to add location tags.
- Keep the caption short and clear.
- Let's post the behind-the-scenes video.
- Let's follow the latest trends.
- Try using trending hashtags.
- That reel format is going viral now.
- The algorithm favors consistency.
- Let's post at peak engagement times.

- We can join a social media challenge.
- Use emojis to make captions lively.
- Let's go live this weekend.
- Polls increase engagement on stories.
- Try using interactive stickers.
- Let's use Canva for design.
- Schedule posts using Meta Business Suite.
- We can track insights through analytics tools.
- Let's shorten the link with Bitly.
- Use AI to generate captions.
- Export the data in Excel format.
- Check post performance in Creator Studio.
- The post is pending approval.
- Make sure the content follows the brand guidelines.
- Let's publish it right after client confirmation.

Identifying and Solving Customer Problem

- Hello, this is Steve from Lavish Technology.
  How can I help you?
- Could you explain the issue you are facing in detail?
- When did this problem first occur?
- Is this happening on all devices or only on one?
- Are you receiving any error messages?
- Can you read the error code for me?
- Does this problem happen consistently or intermittently?
- Are you the only user affected by this issue?
- Have you made any recent changes to your system?
- Did you install any updates before the problem started?
- Can you show me the screen where the issue appears?

- Are you connected to a VPN or any network when the error occurs?
- Is the application freezing or crashing?
- Does this happen during a particular task or action?
- Are other applications running when this problem occurs?
- Is the internet connection stable on your side?
- Can you try logging out and logging in again?
- Have you tried restarting the system?
- Are you getting any pop-up messages?
- Is the software version up to date?
- Are there any warning lights or notifications?
- Can you describe any recent changes to your hardware?
- Did the issue occur after installing new software?
- Are multiple users reporting the same problem?
- Could you provide me access to check the system remotely?
- Let's try clearing the cache first.
- Can you restart the application and try again?
- I suggest checking your internet connection.
- Let's see if the issue happens in another browser.
- Can you check the network cables?
- Try rebooting your device once.
- I will run a diagnostic tool to find the cause.
- Let's update the software to the latest version.
- Can you temporarily disable the firewall and check?
- I will check the server logs for errors.
- Let's reset your password and try logging in.
- Can you uninstall and reinstall the application?
- Try accessing the system from another device.
- I suggest running a virus/malware scan.

- Let's check the storage space on your system.
- I will escalate this to our network team.
- Try disabling any recently installed plugins.
- Let's check if the system time and date are correct.
- Can you share a screenshot of the issue?
- I will provide step-by-step instructions to fix this.
- Let's check your permissions in the system.
- I recommend clearing temporary files.
- Can you test the connection with a different network?
- Let's verify if the latest updates were installed successfully.
- I will guide you through advanced settings to troubleshoot.
- Our team is currently investigating the issue.
- We have identified the root cause of the problem.
- The fix is being implemented now.
- We expect this to be resolved within [time].
- I will keep you updated on the progress.
- The technical team is working on it as a priority.
- The system should be back online shortly.
- We have applied a temporary workaround.
- We are waiting for confirmation from the server team.
- Your ticket has been assigned to a senior engineer.
- The developers are currently testing the solution.
- I have escalated the issue to our cloud team.
- A patch will be released soon to fix this problem.
- The backup system is running while we resolve this.
- We have scheduled a maintenance window for this fix.
- Our support team will contact you once it's resolved.
- We are monitoring the system to prevent recurrence.
- The logs indicate a network outage, and we are fixing it.

- Our engineers are reviewing the error codes.
- We are coordinating with the third-party vendor.
- The fix requires a server restart, which is in progress.
- I have forwarded your issue to the product team.
- The resolution has been verified and applied.
- You should now be able to access the application.
- Please confirm if the issue still persists on your side.
- We apologize for the inconvenience caused.
- Thank you for your patience while we fix this.
- Your feedback is important to us.
- We regret the delay in resolving your issue.
- Thank you for reporting this problem.
- We appreciate your understanding.
- Please let us know if you face further issues.
- We are committed to resolving this as soon as possible.
- I will personally follow up with you once resolved.
- Thank you for bringing this to our attention.
- We apologize for any disruption this may have caused.
- Your ticket has been successfully closed.
- Please confirm that everything is working fine now.
- We value your business and your patience.
- If you experience this again, please contact us immediately.
- We aim to prevent this from happening in the future.
- I will send a summary of the resolution to your email.
- We have noted this for further improvements.
- Thank you for cooperating during the troubleshooting process.
- We have escalated your feedback to the relevant team.
- Your issue has been prioritized for quick resolution.
- Please reach out to me if you have any questions.

- We will continue monitoring to ensure stability.
- We understand the impact and are addressing it urgently.
- Thank you for trusting us with your technical support.
- We hope your system is functioning smoothly now.

General Questions

- Can you introduce yourself?
- What programming languages are you skilled in?
- How do you handle project deadlines?
- What are your strengths as a developer?
- How do you stay updated with new technologies?
- Have you worked on cloud technologies?
- What version control tools do you use?
- How do you handle pressure at work?
- What's your favourite project so far?
- How do you approach debugging complex issues?
- How do you collaborate in a remote team?
- Have you ever managed a team?
- How do you handle client communication?
- What's your experience with Agile or Scrum?
- How do you ensure data security in your project?
- How do you deal with conflicts in a team?
- Have you ever worked with international clients?
- What's your future career goal in IT?
- Why did you choose the IT field?
- What motivates you to learn new technologies?
- What project are you currently working on?
- Which technologies do you use in your team?

- Can you explain your role in this project?
- How do you handle tight deadlines?
- What challenges are you facing in your current project?
- How do you manage code reviews?
- How often do you have sprint meetings?
- What tools do you use for project management?
- How do you ensure code quality?
- Can you explain your testing process?
- Which cloud platform do you work on?
- How do you deploy your applications?
- What CI/CD tools do you use?
- How do you monitor your production environment?
- What's your approach to infrastructure automation?
- How do you handle server downtime?
- How do you manage configuration files?
- Do you use containers or virtual machines?
- What's your experience with Kubernetes?
- How do you handle scaling issues?
- Which programming languages do you prefer?
- How do you handle code conflicts in Git?
- How do you plan your development tasks?
- What's your debugging process?
- How do you test your code before release?
- Do you follow Agile methodology?
- How do you handle client requirements?
- What's your favorite IDE or editor?
- How do you collaborate with other developers?
- How do you document your code?
- How do you optimize performance?

- What's your approach to security in development?
- How do you handle API integration?
- Can you explain your database structure?
- How do you back up your data?
- What's your experience with version control?
- How do you handle software updates?
- What's your approach to error handling?
- How do you ensure cross-browser compatibility?
- What tools do you use for testing?
- Can you share the project status update?
- When can we expect the next deliverable?
- Are there any blockers from your side?
- What are the client's main priorities?
- Can we schedule a demo this week?
- Do you need any support from the client?
- How do you manage client feedback?
- What's the current progress on the feature?
- When will the testing be completed?
- Can you share the deployment plan?
- What is the main objective of this project?
- Who is leading this module?
- How many team members are working on this feature?
- What is the current sprint goal?
- How do you prioritize your tasks?
- Is this issue fixed in the latest build?
- Can we push this update to production?
- How long will it take to complete the integration?
- What are the dependencies for this task?
- Do you have the latest version of the code?

- What is the estimated delivery date?
- Are we following the same design pattern?
- Can you check the bug in the test environment?
- Is the feature working as expected?
- Have you created a pull request?
- Who is reviewing your code?
- Is there any blocker for deployment?
- Can we merge the branch now?
- Is this part automated or manual?
- What's the backup plan if this fails?
- What error are you getting in the console?
- Is the server responding properly?
- Can you restart the service once?
- Have you checked the logs?
- Is this issue reproducible in all browsers?
- What's the root cause of the issue?
- Is the API returning the correct response?
- Can you clear the cache and try again?
- Is this problem from the frontend or backend?
- Have you verified the database connection?
- Is the network stable right now?
- Did you try running the command with admin rights?
- Is this a configuration or coding issue?
- Can you share a screenshot of the error?
- What's the version of the library you are using?
- Have you updated all dependencies?
- Is there any memory leak in the application?
- Can you reproduce the issue locally?
- Have you rolled back the previous changes?

- Is the system working after deployment?
- How satisfied are you with the current progress?
- Would you like any changes in the design?
- Can you please confirm the requirements?
- When can we have the next feedback session?
- Should we include this feature in phase one?
- Do you have any new business requirements?
- Can you share your testing report?
- Are there any priority tasks to be handled first?
- Would you like us to prepare a demo?
- Can we schedule the next meeting on Friday?
- Do you need any performance improvements?
- Are you happy with the user interface?
- Should we integrate payment options now?
- What's your expected delivery timeline?
- Can we close the current milestone?
- Do you want a detailed report this week?
- Is there any critical bug reported from your end?
- Would you like a walkthrough of the system?
- How soon do you need this change implemented?
- Do you have any security concerns?

General IT Conversation

- Can you please check the system issue?
  Sure, I will look into it right away.

- The server is down. What should we do?
  Let's inform the IT support team and check the backup system.

- How long will the software update take?
  It should take around 20 minutes to complete.

- Is the project deployment completed?
  Yes, it's successfully deployed on the production server.

- Can you share the credentials for the test environment?
  Sure, I will send them to you securely via email.

- The computer is running slow. What should I do?
  Try restarting it or closing unnecessary programs.

- The internet is not working. What can be the reason?
  It might be due to a router issue or weak network signal.

- My system is hanging. What should I do?
  Restart the system and check for updates or viruses.

- Can you please reset my password?
  Sure, I will reset it and send you the new one securely.

- The printer is not responding. What should I do?
  Check the connection or reinstall the printer driver.

- Can you check the system log?
  Yes, I will review the logs and identify the issue.

- How do you handle system errors?
  I analyze the cause and apply troubleshooting steps.

- What do you do if an application crashes?
  Restart it, check for bugs, or reinstall the software.

- What should we do if the server goes down?
  Inform the IT admin and switch to backup servers.

- How do you ensure data backup?
  We use cloud storage or scheduled backup systems regularly.

- What project are you working on now?
  I am working on a cloud migration project.

- Which technology are you using?
  We are using AWS and Python for backend development.

- What's your role in this project?
  I am responsible for backend development and API integration.

- How long have you been working in IT?
  I have been working in IT for about five years.

- Do you work from home or office?
  I work in a hybrid model - two days in the office and three from home.

- What's the status of your project?
  The project is in the testing phase now.

- When is the deadline for this module?
  The deadline is next Friday.

- Did you face any issues during development?
  Yes, there were a few API response delays, but we fixed them.

- Who is leading this project?
  Our project manager, Mr. Rajesh, is leading it.

- How do you track project progress?
  We use Jira to track tasks and progress.

- Can you please join the meeting at 10 a.m.?
  Sure, I will be there on time.

- Did you update the task status?
  Yes, I updated it on Jira yesterday.

- Could you review my code?
  Yes, I will check it after lunch.

- Are you done with the testing part?
  Almost, just a few test cases are pending.

- Can we deploy it today?
  Yes, once the QA team gives approval.

- Have you received the client's feedback?
  Yes, the client requested a few UI changes.

- When is the next client call scheduled?
  It's scheduled for tomorrow at 4 p.m.

- How do you handle client issues?
  We respond quickly and provide solutions within 24 hours.

- What did the client say about the last demo?
  The client was satisfied with the performance improvements.

- Can you send the client a report?
  Sure, I will prepare and send it by evening.

- Why is the server down?
  It's due to a maintenance update. It'll be up soon.

- Is the database connection working now?
  Yes, we fixed the issue this morning.

- Can you restart the system once?
  Sure, I will restart and check.

- Did you check the error logs?
  Yes, the logs show a configuration error.

- How do you resolve network issues?
  We first check the router, then the firewall settings.

- How is the progress of your module?
  It's 90% complete, only testing is pending.

- Did you complete the sprint tasks?
  Yes, all sprint tasks are completed and updated in Jira.

- How do you manage project timelines?
  We plan tasks in sprints and monitor through daily stand-ups.

- Who is responsible for code deployment?
  The DevOps team handles the deployment.

- What's the next step after testing?
  Once testing is done, we'll move to production deployment.

- Which cloud service are you using?
  We are using AWS for hosting and storage.

- How do you handle server load?
  We use auto-scaling and load balancers.

- Is the CI/CD pipeline working fine?
  Yes, it's running without errors.

- What tools do you use for deployment?
  We use Jenkins and Docker for continuous deployment.

- Did you check the cloud logs for errors?
  Yes, I reviewed them — no major issues found.

- What framework are you using for frontend?
  We are using React JS for the frontend.

- How do you ensure code quality?
  We follow code reviews and unit testing practices.

- Did you push your changes to Git?
  Yes, I pushed them to the main branch.

- How often do you merge code?
  We merge code at the end of every sprint.

- What version control system do you use?
  We use GitHub for version control.

- What did you do yesterday?
  I completed the login module and fixed a few bugs.

- What are you planning to do today?
  I will start working on the payment gateway integration.

- Do you have any blockers?
  Yes, I am waiting for the API documentation from the client.

- Can we discuss the new requirements?
  Sure, let's schedule a short meeting.

- Who will handle the next sprint tasks?
  The new team members will take care of that.

- Is the testing completed?
  Yes, functional and regression testing are done.

- Did you find any critical bugs?
  Yes, two high-priority bugs were found during testing.

- How do you report bugs?
  We log them in Jira with screenshots and steps to reproduce.

- Who verifies the bug fixes?
  The QA team verifies them after developers resolve issues.

- When will we get the QA report?
  You will receive it by tomorrow morning.

- How was the client meeting?
  It went well; they approved the new UI design.

- What feedback did the client give?
  They suggested improving the page loading speed.

- How do you prepare for client demos?
  We test all features and create a clear presentation flow.

- Did the client approve the final version?
  Yes, they approved it without any changes.

- What's the client's priority now?
  They want to focus on mobile app optimization.

Subject	Verb Present	Verb Past
I	am	was
He	is	was
She	is	was
It	is	was
We	are	were
You	are	were
They	are	were
He	has	had
She	has	had
It	has	had
I	have	had
We	have	had
You	have	had
They	have	had
I	do	did
We	do	did
You	do	did
They	do	did
He	does	did
She	does	did
It	does	did

Singular	Plural
I am	We are
You are	You are
He/She/It is	They are

Singular	Plural
I was.	We were.
You were.	You were.
He/She/It was.	They were.

Singular	Plural
I have	-
He has	We have
She has	You have
It has	They have

Singular	Plural
I have been.	We have been.
You have been.	You have been.
He/She/It has been.	They have been.

Singular	Plural
I had been.	We had been.
You had been.	You had been.
He/She/It had been.	They had been.

	Singular	Plural
First Person (The person speaking)	I, me, my, mine	We, us, our, ours
Second Person (The person spoken to)	You, your, yours	You, your, yours
Third Person (The person or thing being spoken about)	He, him, his, she, her hers, it, its	They, them, their, theirs

1st person	I	Me	My	Mine	Myself
2nd person	You	You	Your	Yours	Yourself
3rd Person (male)	He	Him	His	His	Himself
3rd Person (female)	She	Her	Her	Hers	Herself
3rd thing	It	It	Its	-	Itself
1st person (plural)	We	Us	Our	Ours	Ourselves
2nd person (plural)	You	You	Your	Yours	Yourselves
3rd person & thing (plural)	They	Them	Their	Theirs	themselves